Dancing
In The Storm

Dancing In The Storm

Jennifer M Killby

Writers Club Press
San Jose New York Lincoln Shanghai

Dancing In The Storm

Writers Club Press
an imprint of iUniverse.com, Inc.

For information address:
iUniverse.com, Inc.
5220 S 16th, Ste. 200
Lincoln, NE 68512
www.iuniverse.com

Names of individuals involved have been changed for their privacy and protection.

ISBN: 0-595-18646-7

Printed in the United States of America

Dedicated to my Father,
the God of all creation.

This book was written in loving memory of the people who have helped
me get to the place I am in God.

Sister Pamela Fletcher
Evangelist Patricia Ferrell
Sister Sherri Mouton
Bishop Arthur L. Fletcher
Deacon Capus McCall
Brother Kortardra Blount

You have all helped me shoulder my burdens and grow in God.
I thank you!

I want to also thank everyone else involved in my life. You have taught me
more than you could ever imagine.
I love you all, especially you Grandpa!

God Bless every one of you!!!

"Have pity upon me, have pity upon me, O ye friends; for the hand of God hath touched me. Why do ye persecute me as God, and are not satisfied with my flesh? Oh that my words were written! Oh that they were printed in a book! That they were graven with an iron pen and lead in the rock for ever!"

— Job 19:21-24

PREFACE

"And I thank Jesus Christ our Lord, who hath enabled me, for that he counted me faithful, putting me into ministry; Who was before a blasphemer, and persecutor, and injurious: But I obtained mercy, because I did it ignorantly in unbelief. And the grace of our Lord was exceeding abundant with faith and love which is in Jesus Christ. This is a faithful saying, and worthy of all acceptance, that Christ Jesus came into the world to save sinners; of whom I am chief."

-First Timothy 1:12-15

I thank God he chose to pull me from the world. I thank God he felt compassion for someone who could have cared less whether He existed or not. I thank God he thought of me as a person when I had become nothing. I thank God he found me and brought me safely to the fold. Without him, I do not know where I would be.

ACKNOWLEDGEMENTS

All Biblical scripture used in this book was taken from the King James Version of the Holy Bible.

LIST OF CONTRIBUTORS

PATRICIA FERRELL, Evangelist, Superintendent of Sunday School for Calvary Christian Pentecostal Church of Pensacola, Florida, Devoted elementary school teacher.

CHAPTER ONE

"*Train up a child in the way he should go:*
And when he old he will not depart from it."

Proverbs 22:6

****

A father let his child walk a path that was on their property daily. The father walked the path as a child and knew it well. He instructed his son about the path and even walked the path with his son a few times to make sure he understood his instructions. One day as the child walked the path alone he noticed something in the distance that attracted his curiosity. The child debated within himself whether or not he should leave the path. When he could not contain himself any longer, he stepped off the path. The child took great care to watch where he was going. He often looked back to make sure he did not venture too far from the path. The closer he walked toward the object, the further away in seemed. Before the child knew it, he ventured too far away from the path. The path was lost behind the mass of trees and shrubs. He was lost. He became frightened when he noticed the sun slowly descending into the western sky. He fell to his knees crying. His first thoughts were that his father would be furious with him.

Back at the house, his father had settled in for the evening on the back porch. He sat there every evening to watch his son's smiling face as he emerged from the wooded path, but this time something was wrong. His son had not returned, and it was growing late. Just as the father arose to his feet to look for his son, he heard a faint cry.

"Help me! I'm lost!" His son, he thought to himself. The father ran into the woods to look for his son.

"Where are you," the father yelled?

"I don't know! I'm lost!" The boy was in a thicket and could not discern where he was. The father patiently looked for the boy talking to him as he looked. He was able to keep his son calm by talking with him. He knew deep down the only way he would be able to find his son would be by the sound of his voice. After a few minutes the father finally found his son. The father ran to the boy. He grabbed him into his arms and hugged him. They walked back to the path together.

Our Father, God in Heaven, has done the same thing for us. God gave us instructions on how we should live. It is up to us to follow his instruction and stay on the correct path or disregard his instruction altogether.

> *"O that there were such an heart in them,*
> *That they would fear me,*
> *And keep all my commandments always,*
> *That it might be well with them,*
> *And with there children forever!"*

> Deuteronomy 5:29

Occasionally, in life, we are attracted to something that will lead us off our chosen path if we allow it to.

> *"For we ourselves were sometimes foolish,*
> *Disobedient, deceived, serving divers lusts*
> *And pleasures, living in malice and envy,*
> *Hateful, and hating one another."*

Titus 3:3

When we come to realize that we are lost, all we need to do is cry out for our Father in Heaven.

> *"The Lord is nigh unto them that are of a broken heart;*
> *And saveth such as be of a contrite spirit."*

Psalm 34:18

We have a loving Father who waits for us to come home to him. He knows we are in trouble before we even realize something is wrong.

> *"And it shall come to pass, that before they call,*
> *I will answer;*
> *And while they are yet speaking,*
> *I will hear."*

Isaiah 65:24

God will go out and look for us, find us and deliver us from our circumstance.

> *"Though I walk in the midst of trouble,*
> *Thou wilt revive me:*
> *Thou shalt stretch forth thine hand*

Against the wrath of mine enemies,
And thy right hand shall save me."

Psalms 138:7

God is faithful to forgive us of our sins and walk us back to the correct path towards home.

"But if the wicked will turn from all his sins
That he hath committed, and keep all my statutes,
And do that which is lawful and right,
He shall not die.
All his transgressions that he committed,
They shall not be mentioned unto him:
In his righteousness that he hath done he shall live."

Ezekiel 18:21, 22

Are you walking on the right path or have you strayed from it?

****

Has it ever crossed you mind, "Why me?" Have you ever wondered
why the world is constantly kicking you around and you cannot see any
relief in sight? Have you ever asked God, "Why?" Have you ever wondered why God would even let anything bad ever happen to you? Did
you become angry with God, and walk further from him? Did you ever
feel God did not love you? Did you feel God slammed a door in your
face you could not open? These are normal emotions for people who
have had one tragedy after another befall them. Our emotions are a tool
God has given us to express ourselves. However, our emotions should
not be used to determine the outcome of events in our lives. Emotions
cloud logic. Sometimes we get angry or upset because the event that

took place was something we did not want to happen. It was out of our control. It went against our "perfect world theology". The first one we blame is God. It is easier to believe God does not love us. It is easier to believe God did it on purpose out of contempt. It is easier to blame God for what happens in our lives, because it would kill us to blame ourselves for our own actions.

We all have asked the questions, but have we honestly waited for the answers? God has answered each one of us daily, but we chose to ignore Him. The answers just did not suit what we wanted to hear. The world had better answers. They came quicker and offered better results. I chose to believe the world's point of view, also. I chose to believe I had control over my life even though I did not care whether I lived or died. I believed I knew what was best for me. God was only getting in my way. I did not want what God offered. I felt it was too good to be true. I truly believe that is why God will let us bask in our own ignorance until we have had enough. God knows how to bring us to our knees. He knows when we have been in the fire long enough. Some of us probably have wished we had listened to him earlier. I can actually see the moments in my life where God was trying to help me and I turned Him away. I see the moments in my life where the world was trying to check me out and God stepped in and said, "No!" It is heartbreaking, now, to actually know that when I thought no one cared, God was holding me in his arms the whole time.

If anyone could have been further from God, it would have been me. I was not given the opportunity to now God through my family. My family had a respect for God, but that was all. I upheld God like you would a person of honor. In fact, the bible I received as an Easter gift when I was a child was treated like as a precious gem. Up until present, that was the only relationship I ever had with God. I thank God that he had the patience to wait on me. I thank God that even though I did not acknowledge him in my daily life, he saw and acknowledged me. I thank God that he met every need I ever had through the years.

My memories of my life go back to the age of two. I believe the memories I have were kept in tack for a reason. Believe me, they are not good memories. My early childhood memories of my father only strengthened my beliefs that men were creatures more than they were human. I don't recall having any kind of bond with my father.

My mother and father married young and I was born a year later. My sister joined the family about two years after me. My memories of my father had always been of fear. I remember him being a strict disciplinarian. Sometimes my mom had to intervene to keep him from punishing us for something trivial. I felt I had to walk around as quiet as a mouse to avoid him.

My father used the fad drugs of the seventies, which made his behavior erratic. I do not know if he ever hurt my mother. On one occasion, I remember my father screaming that the devil was after him. My mother swept us out of the house and took us to another location. She did not take us out fast enough. To this day, I can see my father sitting in the middle of the living room floor holding a shotgun in his hands. His face looked distorted. As a child the scene haunted me for a long time. Now, it is just one of the countless memories I wish I could forget.

My mother and father divorced about the time I was four years of age. My mother never spoke about my father. I did not hear from my father for almost eight years. He had started a life in California with a new wife. The letters lasted for a little while then they stopped. I never asked why my mother and he got a divorce. I chose to ignore the questions at the time. On one occasion, I over heard a group of my mom's friends and her talking about my father and how he dedicated his life back to God. I also remember them laughing about it. I thought in my heart he had changed for the good. However, the constant attacks against my mother showed me that he had not. I learned that it is all right to lye down your religion when it suited you. I talk to my father to this day. Our relationship still needs some mending. I just have to learn to love him with the very same love that it took for Jesus to die on the cross. I can only hope that my father will someday hand his life over to God.

My mom, sister and I moved in with my grandparents after my mother's separation from my father. My grandparents offered the solid foundation my sister and I never had. It was perfect except for one thing. My mother worked two jobs to pay off some debt from the marriage. My mom also enjoyed going out with her friends, a lot. I was never upset with my mom for working two jobs. I knew it had to be done. I became upset with her when she only had to work one job and still chose to stay away from the house. I can remember days when all I wanted was for her to spend time with my sister and I. We would beg her to say at home with us. She would just smile, hug my sister and I, and walk out the door. I learned from my mother that I could do what I wanted without regard for my children's feelings or anyone else's for that matter.

My mother was a woman of strong opinion and spoke her mind. I did not understand her, but I just trusted everything she said. Sometimes, she would hurt my feelings with some of the thing she would say. I would just shrug it off and go on with my day. Sometimes I thought she was just trying to toughen me up. I was very shy. I know my shyness kept me from doing things that would benefit me. However, there was one thing she said I would never forget. I can remember the exact moment as if it were frozen in memory. She was ironing clothes. I was watching television. Out of the blue she started talking about suicide.

"Suicide is a sin. You'll go straight to hell, if you commit suicide." I looked at her and smiled. I said nothing in return. I remember her words being carved into my memory. At the time, I could not understand why she had said it, but I am glad she did. My mother was not the type of person to talk about religious matters. I know, now, God used my mother to send me a warning.

My mom used very few words to express herself. I cannot remember, as a child, having more than a two-minute conversation with her. As I became an adult, the conversations improved very little. We would talk except about things that really mattered. I could never tell her how I felt or what was really going on in my life. We never had a strong emotional bond. I just chose to lie to her to avoid answering her questions. I became very good at lying to people to avoid telling the truth. Telling the truth meant I had to face what I had done. Telling the truth meant I was not as perfect as I thought I was. Lying helped me create the world I wanted to live in.

I loved my mother. I adored her. She was the perfect role model of a strong independent woman. All I ever wanted was to be like her. As I became older, I focused my attention on her likes and dislikes. If my mom liked it, I liked it. If my mom disliked something, I disliked it, also. My mom saw this in me. She would often tell me to form my own opinions. I did not want to do that. Why forge my own personality. Hers was perfectly fine to me. I look back, now, and see how big of a mistake I had made. I never explored who I really was, and when I finally had to, I fell flat on my face.

My grandmother was very different from my mother. She was soft spoken. Her feelings were easily hurt. I thought of her as a weak person. I did not understand her weaknesses were her strongest attributes. I did not understand that a woman did not have to be pushy or loud spoken to achieve her goals. I did not understand a woman could achieve her goals and still maintain her attributes as a lady. My grandmother dedicated her life to her family. She held firm to her beliefs. Things like, "It is not proper for a young lady to act overly flirtatious with a young boy. It is not proper for a young lady to carry herself as a man would. It is not proper for a young lady to talk to more than one boy at a time." These and a book of others were recited to me quite often through my teen years. She let me know it when I stepped out of bounds. Of course, I never thought she was being fair. I felt she was trying to enforce prehistoric codes of conduct on my life.

"It's the 80"s. People don't do that any more," I would say in defense.

"It's my house," she would refute. My grandmother's father was a preacher. I did not know that until my adult life. I often wondered why she never went to church. She always spoke about doing good and what was right, but I never knew where she got her information. This is another place in my life where my ideologies became confused. I learned I did not have to go to church to be saved. What really amazed me was how my family said to do the right thing, but never taught by example. I did not know what the right this was. I just followed the examples they showed me.

I can say one thing. The relationship between my grandmother and grandfather was a good example of a Godly marriage. My grandmother and grandfather had what I would call a "perfect" relationship. They never argued in front of anyone. They had grown so close that they functioned as one. Who would not have with my grandfather? He is one of the last true gentlemen left of this planet. He always reminded me of a teddy bear. I always felt safe around him. For a man to live with five women day in and day out he had to be strong in his stance as a man. Not once did he ever blow-up or lose his patience openly. He was truly a patient man. He endured five different perfumes, hair sprays, attitudes, and only two bathrooms that were occupied the majority of the day.

I tried to compare other men to him, but no one ever measured up. I always settled for far less. Quite honestly, at the time, I did not think it would be hard to find a man like him. I thought it was natural for a man to act in that manner. My grandfather was like my grandmother. He dedicated his entire life to his family. He worked hard everyday. He instilled work values that would pay off in later years. The only time I thought my grandfather was vulnerable was when my grandmother passed away a few years ago. I saw my grandfather as my grandmother did. I saw him as the man that loved her. I saw a man who just lost a life partner. My grandmother's death did not bother me as much as seeing my grandfather in the condition he was in.

My childhood, after the divorce of my parents was fairly good. My mom and grandparents made sure my sister and I had whatever we wanted within reason. This also meant that we had plenty of things to keep us busy amongst ourselves. My sister and I had wonderful imaginations. We put ourselves in different worlds. We created things to do.

When I was six years of age, I helped teach my sister to read and write. My sister and I went to Sunday school all the time. I can only remember a few times that my mother attended church with us. I loved church. During vacation bible school, I received a reward for bringing the most people to church. I forgot what age I actually was, but I remember I was still in elementary school when I had invited Jesus to come into my heart. I was thrilled. I could not wait to get home to tell my mom. I thought she would be happy. When I got home and told my mom the news, she just looked at me. I felt I had done something wrong. The significance of it was made small and useless. I slowly stopped going to church and started studying the occult.

My sister and I were close until I hit my teen years. Our relationship barely existed after that point. We only spoke when we had to. We just coexisted with each other. My friends became more important to me. It was not until later in life, I found out that the same demons that haunted me in high school haunted her. We both had suffered similar events and neither one of us knew. My family was very good at keeping things quiet. Anything that would be a disgrace was disguised or hidden. This became a catalyst to several years of abuse I did not have to suffer.

Independence became my enemy. The older I got the less I felt I needed my family. I withdrew from them. My freshman year of high school actually showed me how much support my family had for me. I had become extremely depressed. The reason is still a mystery to me.

Nothing tragic had happened. There was no change is my family structure. Everything was the same as it was a year earlier. I saw a psychiatrist
at school. He talked to me for a while and had me draw some pictures.
He asked me questions about the pictures and that was it. No one ever
told me what his conclusions were. I heard speculation that the cause of
my depression was from not wanting to grow up and high school meant
I had to. Personally, I was thrilled to be in high school. By the time summer vacation came, I felt I was doing better. The problem had only been
masked. I learned how to bury it deep down inside of myself. I knew my
teen years were supposed to be fun and I was not going to let pills and
doctors get in my way.

I continued on with high school in full throttle. I became my mom's
worst nightmare just like any other teen girl. I hung out with my friends
most of the time and the rest of the time I kept the phones busy with
boys calling. I was never really aloud to go on a date until I was well into
my sixteenth year. That did not keep me from sneaking and seeing my
boyfriends at my friends' houses or at their houses. My mom would
only let me go out once a week and that was limited. I had to be back
early depending on where I was going. In my sophomore year of high
school, I met a young man that lived thirty miles from me. I only got to
see him about twice a week and I was barely aloud to go anywhere with
him. We hit it off from the beginning. We wrote letters back and forth to
each other. He had joined the Air force before we met and was scheduled to leave the summer before my junior year. I was thrilled when he
asked me to go to his prom. However, my mom was not. After days of
begging and my boyfriend's mother calling, she finally agreed to let me
go. I am happy she did. If my mom would not had let me go, I would
not have gone to any proms throughout high school. After he left for the
air force, he and his mom insisted on me dating while he was gone.
They wanted me to be sure I really wanted to be with him. It would be
one time that I would ever regret listening to someone.

I joined the army in my junior year of high school. I was surprised my mother let me join. I was only seventeen. She signed the papers with no problem. The summer between my junior and senior year I went to boot camp. I did not like it. I had hurt my back early in boot camp and had a very difficult time. I did manage to finish boot camp. I came home a week or so before my senior year of high school. My boyfriend and I still wrote each other. I started dating other guys casually. My decision to date other guys had a negative impact on the next twelve years of my life. On December 25, 1987, I met the man that would change my life so cruelly that the effects of it would last for ten years after the relationship ended.

From the beginning my family did not like my new boyfriend. That was a green light for me. I ignored the signs that were right in front of my face. He went into fits of rage. I ignored them. I just thought they were merely temper tantrums. I did not understand how dangerous they would become. Anthony manipulated my time. He wanted me around him constantly. His insistence on seeing me led me to lie to my mom about baby-sitting so I could see him. The devil invited me to dinner and I graciously accepted his invitation. I could not even enjoy my graduation. Anthony persuaded me that it would not be a good idea for me to hang around my friends. They would only be a bad influence on me. Plus he felt I drank too much and going to any graduation parties would make my drinking worse. I became furious. I could not believe he had the nerve to tell me what to do. He pouted until I finally gave in.

When it came time for me to leave to finish my final training for the army, Anthony convinced me not to go. I resigned from the army. My family was furious. They started to verbally attack Anthony. I, of course, ignored them and continued to date him. Anthony became more possessive. He gradually grew physically aggressive toward me. The August after I graduated from high school I moved in with him and his parents. After two weeks I landed a good job with a trucking firm. Two weeks later I called my mom and asked her to help me move out. My mom borrowed her company's truck and helped me gather my belongings. The whole time Anthony was on the roof of the house threatening to commit suicide. My mother laughed at him and asked me how I could date such an immature person. I ignored her. I had lost respect for Anthony. I knew he had problems. My problem was loneliness. It was something I did not want to live with. No more than two weeks later, I was back with him and in November of the same year we moved into an apartment together. I chose to be in a bad relationship instead of waiting for a good one to come my way.

The apartment was thirty miles from my family. I loved being in my own place. I felt I had achieved something. I chose to deal with the cruel behavior that Anthony displayed toward me. I figured it could not get any worse. I was wrong. It was not long before he became increasingly violent toward me. I was caught in his snare. It was easy for him to pull me away from my family. I already did not have a strong bond with them and he used this to make me believe they did not want me around them due to the fact I was with him. He would often tell me he did not feel comfortable going over to my grandparent's house. I was able to sympathize with him, because of how I believed my family was. My eyes were closed to what was really happening. He had the advantage over me. I was thirty miles from home and we did not have a phone. I was going to college full-time while working forty hours a week. My family did not think anything was out of the ordinary. They just assumed I was too busy to see them. I began to slip and I had no one to catch me. My pride had a lot to do with my decisions. I thought if I had gone back home, my family would have won. I could not let them think I was a failure. My pride blinded me. To stay with Anthony was a decision that could have cost me my life.

> *"Pride goeth before destruction,*
> *And a haughty spirit before a fall."*

Proverbs 16:18

CHAPTER TWO

****

A young woman sat at her window and watched a storm blow in. It cast a dark shadow over everything. Without notice the rain plummeted down. The lightning tore through the sky's canvas. The wind bent the strongest trees and the thunder screamed in her ears. Thinking the storm would only last a little while she canceled her plans for the day. When she awoke the next morning, the storm was still tearing at her home. The woman was fearful of the storm. She was too frightened to go out into the midst of it. She became a prisoner in her own home.

After a week the storm still raged outside. The woman gathered the courage she needed to go outside. She walked over to her front door and opened it. She stood there watching intently as the rain pelted the soaked ground. She watched in horror as the lightning ripped holes in the darkness. She watched the strongest trees bend in the wind's persistence. She closed her eyes. Trembling she placed one foot outside. Then she placed the other outside. She took one step, two steps, three steps, four and then five. Before she knew it, she was standing in the middle of her front yard.

The woman smiled and then started laughing. She realized that no matter how hard the rain fell, the lightning lit the sky, or how hard the wind blew, it could not stop her from going outside. Her fear was gone. She began to dance. She jumped and leaped for joy. She laughed and sang. She knew she conquered the storm.

No matter how hard we try to avoid trouble in our lives, it will always be there.

> *"Although affliction cometh not forth of the dust, neither doth trouble spring out of the ground; Yet man is born unto trouble, as sparks fly upward."*

> Job 5:6,7

The question is, do you hide from your troubles or face them? We have no excuses. God gives us strength to face them. We have to step out in faith into the middle of the storm.

> *"God is our refuge and strength,*
> *A very present help in trouble.*
> *Therefore will not we fear,*
> *Though the earth be removed,*
> *And though the mountains*
> *Be carried away into*
> *The midst of the sea..."*

> Psalm 46:1,2

Not only do we need to step out in faith into the storm, but also rejoice knowing that God is perfecting us.

> *"And not only so, but we glory in tribulation also:*
> *Knowing that tribulation worketh patience;*
> *Patience, experience; and experience,*
> *Hope"*

Romans 5:3,4

How many storms have kept you stranded? How many have you conquered?

✽✽✽✽✽✽✽

His hands circled my throat, and he forced me to the floor. I had no choice but to fall under his grip. He sat on top of me. I knew if I resisted it would just anger him more and I might receive more injuries. I was still sore from two days ago. Tears streamed down my cheeks. I dared not to let out a cry even though I was in excruciating pain. When he felt my muscles relax under his grip, he grabbed my hair and began to slam my head into the cement floor. I was about to black out when he stopped. He released his grip and got up from sitting on me. I knew not to move. It would only kindle his rage even more. I closed my eyes and listened for him to walk away. Once I believed he was out of the room, I cautiously got up from the floor. I leaned against the wall until I got my balance. I glanced around to see where he could have gone. I could not see him. I walked back to our bedroom. He was on the bed sleeping. I thought how easy it would be for me to snatch his life from him. Hate began to consume me. I shut the bedroom lights off and walked into the living room. I turned the television on. I flipped through the channels, but nothing seemed to attract my attention. I wanted to go home. I wanted to call my mom. I wanted released from the prison I put myself in. I stretched out on the couch. Thoughts began to interrupt my throbbing headache.

"Why me," I whispered? "What have I done to deserve this?" I was well aware of what was going on. I was too embarrassed to tell anyone. I made a mistake and could not admit it. I did want my family to know they were right. I chose to stay with him. The beatings I received were far more tolerable than hearing "I told you so" from my family. I admit my pride has always been my downfall. I believe, also, the whole wedding stigma had me entranced. It was important for me to be married. I had just told my family I was getting married. I could not back out now. Of course, my family told me to wait a little while longer. I did not want to. If I was going to get married I wanted to do it now. I had already waited until the last moment to tell them. The wedding was planned for May and it was already March. I was surprised when my family made the decision to help with the wedding. I was worried about how it was going to get paid for. I knew Anthony was not going to help with any funds.

The two months before the wedding went quickly. We had the wedding scheduled to be in a rose garden in a park. Nature suggested otherwise. It began to rain the day of the wedding. I was a little upset, but alternative plans had already been made in advance. I was worried some of my out of town guests would get lost, but they all found the church easily. My grandfather took my two bridesmaids and I to the church in his car. My uncle, who was a professional photographer, took the wedding pictures as a wedding gift. I was thrilled that everything else was running smoothly. I was doing fine up until it was time to line up for the wedding procession to walk down the isle. I turned to my grandfather in tears. He hugged me. Inside I begged my grandfather to stop the wedding and take me home. The words never formed in my mouth. I had found out one month earlier that I was pregnant. I could not disappoint my family like that. I had to marry him. I knew I was signing my own death certificate. On May 6, 1989, I sealed my faith for the next eleven years.

For a month or two everything went fine. I began to believe he had changed, but without any warning the violence started again. This time I was his property. My health deteriorated as my pregnancy progressed. The stress on my shoulders was greater than anything I could have imagined. I became disconnected with what was happening. I counteracted with anger. I grew increasingly angry at the people surrounding me for not seeing what was going on or just not doing anything about it. I could feel the person I once knew slowly walk away. I became a different person in order to survive. I let the person who was born out of the constant stress and torture rule my life. The old me was locked away behind bars watching what was going on is disbelief.

My husband was lazy and found ways to keep from working. He often called the paramedics from his job and told them I needed to go to the hospital. Nothing was ever wrong with me. He just wanted to get out of work for the night. I cannot count how many useless trips I made to the hospital. In his own twisted little way, I guess he thought he was doing me a favor. He started pulling money out of the account without telling me resulting in checks being returned for insufficient funds. I could have had him arrested for it, but I did not. I was happy when he started to stay away from the house for extended periods of time. He would tell me not to leave. I often grew tired of waiting and went to the store and spent money I did not have. I knew of his father's infidelity and felt the apple did not fall far from the tree. I just assumed my husband was cheating on me. It really did not bother me. I figured his attention was being taken off of me, and when he became unemployed again, it worked out for the best.

On one occasion, when he was driving home, he got rear ended by another car as he pulled into the parking lot. When he came up to the apartment to tell me, I did not believe him. He had lied to me so many times before about injuries, I just thought this was one of his lies again.

My friend, who was visiting, laughed it off. Even when he picked up the phone to call 911, I still felt he was lying. My friend and I carried on our conversation. He became angry and cursed us out. He left to go outside to wait for the police and ambulance. My friend and I decided to go outside and check out what happened. The police and ambulance arrived a few seconds later. After a report was taken Anthony insisted on going to the hospital. The ambulance took him. My friend and I followed behind. He complained his neck was hurting. I just figured he wanted to get some insurance money out of it. I could have cared less if he was really hurt or not. The incident had interrupted my time with my friend.

I was six months pregnant and did not feel like sitting in a hospital waiting room. After a few hours of waiting, I decided to leave. I went to his room and told him I was going to leave, but he would not let me go. An hour or two later the hospital released him. My friend went home. I asked her to stay, but she did not feel comfortable being around my husband. It would not be until a few years later that I found out that he tried to get into the bathroom while she was taking a shower. She said she had the door locked and she could hear him trying to jimmy the door open. The next day the hospital called and told me to immediately bring him back. He had cracked a few vertebrae in his neck. I waited until after I had ate and took a shower to tell him. I drove him to the hospital. I remember praying that someone would hit me and he would break his neck and die. My husband, in his typical manner, milked the situation. He received a decent settlement from the insurance company a few months later. I used it to pay off some outstanding bills.

I let my standards of living drop to new lows. It was the only way I could consciously allow what was happening to me to go on. I thought it was necessary in order for me to survive. Sometimes this would mean giving into performing degrading acts or permitting him to perform some of his degrading behaviors toward me. I let him believe he had control over everything. I would often go behind him and correct his errors without him knowing. My pregnancy became more high risk the closer I got to my due date. He also became more demanding of me. My doctor had warned him to let me stay off of my feet on several occasions. He always shook his head in agreement. No sooner would we get home, he would complain that the house needed cleaned or that he wanted me to cook for him. I would clean the house and cook just to keep the confusion down to a minimum. The month before my son was born I had to see a podiatrist. My legs had swollen so badly they were affecting my feet. I could barely walk. A week before my due date, the podiatrist took me out of work. I do not know if my husband felt sorry for me or if he just grew weary of treating me so cruelly, but he backed off of me the last week I was pregnant. I was able to relax a little and get some sleep.

The day I went to the hospital to have my first son, I was completely frightened. I called my family. They drove thirty miles to the hospital to see me. The doctor said my contractions were not doing anything. She decided to keep me in the hospital over night.

The doctor said she would induce my labor in the morning if I had not dilated by then. My husband had started a new job a couple weeks earlier, and decided he should go to work. My family went home with the exception of my grandmother. I guess she knew I needed someone to stay with me. She walked with me every hour on the hour up and down the hospital hallway. I felt safe with her. I wanted her to baby me like she use to when I was sick. She expressed that she hoped I would have a boy. She had always wanted a boy. She had three daughters and two granddaughters. My son would be the first boy born into our family after years of girls.

I was frightened of what the next day would bring. My grandmother kept reassuring me that she would not leave me. She stayed the entire night in my room. She would occasionally go out and get some coffee or talk with the nurses. Deep down I hoped that the baby would change Anthony. I knew the reality was far different. I wanted to tell my grandmother everything, but the words never touched my lips. I could not tell her of the horrors I had been through the past year and a half. I knew it would hurt her. I knew she would have saved me from the hell if only I had told her. Sometimes I wondered if she already knew, but just did not say anything. She was so emotional. Her heart was easily broken. I never gathered the strength to tell her.

Early the next morning a nurse came into the room to give me an IV My grandmother had left the room to get some coffee. After the nurse put the needle in my arm she draped the tubing over the edge of the bed facing the floor. The nurse stepped out of the room to do something. She had forgotten to close the cathedar to the needle. I bled openly until she returned. I had lost almost a pint of blood I desperately needed. She closed the cathedar and wiped up the blood without showing any concern for me. I do not believe she was aware I knew what happened. Directly in front of my bed was a full-length mirror. I saw everything that happened. It went downhill from there.

My family slowly filtered back in and my husband straggled in behind them. The doctor came in, induced my labor, broke my water and then left. It took all day for me to dilate. My condition was deteriorating rapidly. I pushed for two hours before the doctor finally came back to see that the baby and I were in distress. She called an emergency c-section. I was so out of it I did not know what was going on. I just wanted everything over with. My husband was getting a high off all the excitement. Of course, he was getting the attention he craved from everyone. After what seemed like hours, they finally rolled me into the operating room. After they prepped me for the surgery, they allowed my husband to come in. I did not want him there. His false concern for me did not fool me.

I had to stay in the hospital a week. I was there during the Thanksgiving holiday. I was upset that no one spent any time with me in the hospital. Everyone enjoyed there Thanksgiving dinners at his or her individual homes. My grandmother had informed me while I was in the hospital that upon finding out I was having a boy, my husband told her that her baby boy had been born. She said I might as well go on and hand him over to her. The doctor did not want me to leave when it was time. I had acquired an infection from the surgery. I begged her to let me go home. She explained to my husband that I needed plenty of rest. He told her he would make sure I received plenty. She released me. My aunt volunteered to help me until I could get around good on my own. My husband did not lend one helping hand toward my aunt or I. Not once did he get up with the baby or feed him. My aunt and I did it all. He often yelled at me telling me to get off my fat butt and stop being so lazy. My aunt was only able to take a few days of it and left. I was by myself again. She was the only thing keeping him off of me. I understood why she had left. I probably would have done the same thing. Deep down I hoped she would tell someone.

After six weeks I returned to work. I also started attending a technical college that was close by. My grandparents kept my son for me while I was working and going to school. I only got to see my son on the weekends. My mother-in-law had volunteered to watch him. Even though she was closer, I did not feel comfortable with her watching him. Her overall negative attitude toward everyone and the fact that she worked the night shift kept me from exploring the idea any further. I felt safer knowing my son was far away from my husband. It made it hard for my husband to get him. The beatings were getting worse. He often questioned where I was when I came home from school. I grew tired of him questioning me and started firing questions at him. It sent him into rages.

I had grown tired of his behavior and turned it against him. I started playing games with him. I figured I was going to get hit anyhow. Why not make it worth the trouble? I teased him and let false information slip and then try to cover it up. I noticed he started rummaging through my things when I was gone, following me, and calling co-workers to see where I was. I kept the games up until he brought home a .357 magnum. He cleaned and loaded it in front of me almost on a daily basis. He described how deadly the weapon was. I already knew what it could do. I was in the military. I had a great respect for weapons. Sometimes, when we argued, I would tell him he did not have the balls to pull the trigger. He carried the gun wherever he went. When we were in the apartment I made sure I knew where Anthony was at all times. I felt reality slip far from me. I had no defense against a gun. I knew the gun gave him a heightened sense of superiority. I knew he was even more dangerous than he ever had been in the past.

The beatings got worse. At first I was afraid to defend myself. I did not know how he would react with the gun. In order to keep my sanity, I could not just let him hit me anymore. I had to defend myself. I often locked my infant son in his bedroom so he would not get hurt. I got the police department involved. At times they would just laugh at me and say it was just my imagination. I became increasingly angry within myself. One night, after a very intense argument, I was finally awarded my freedom.

"When I get home, I want you and your junk gone," he screamed at me!

"The only piece of trash in this room is you!" The words no more escaped my mouth before I was shoved to the floor. "I guess you feel like a man, now!" One of his work boots connected with my back.

"You are a worthless female dog," he screamed as he walked toward the door!

"At least I'm not the crap that comes from the dog! That's all you'll ever be!" He stopped dead in his tracks. He walked back to where I was. I was still on the floor. I had learned not to get up if I ended up on the floor. He grabbed my hair and shoved my head to the floor.

"You better not be here when I get home." His voice lowered as the words spilled out of his mouth. I took him up on his offer. No more than two minutes after he had left, I called my family to come and help me move. They came without question and helped me leave. I cleared all the bank accounts and went back to my grandparent's house. I left no note. No one in my family ever questioned me as to what happened. I never volunteered the information.

The first few days, weeks, or months after a person leaves an abusive relationship are crucial. It could mean success or failure. In some cases it could mean life or death. My husband was a smooth talker. He convinced me he would change and that he was sorry for what he had done. I reluctantly went back to him. I felt like I had no choice. I believed things could get better. I believed he could change. I wanted to believe he would change. Deep down where it matters, I knew he was not going to change. I could hear a voice begging me not to go back. You know that bad feeling you get when you know you are about to do something wrong, but you do it anyhow? That is the same bad feeling I had. I just ignored it. It reminds me of something my great grandmother once said. "If you have a bad feeling about something and have to think twice about doing it, don't do it." It was advice I should had adhered to, but did not.

Anthony was good to me for a while. He even tried to attend some family functions without complaining. He blamed my family for me leaving. I could see it in his eyes. He was not aware that I did not tell them. He just assumed that I had. I was too embarrassed to tell them, but I let him go on thinking that I told them. I felt I would be safer this way. I could have never been more wrong. It is amazing how people do not even think of the consequences they will suffer from their actions. Anthony was an impulsive person. He believed he owned me. I observed his behavior for a little while, until it got out of hand.

I was more headstrong now and refused to be treated like an animal. I would literally attack him if he even breathed on me wrong. A lot of times he acted out of self-defense. More than a few times the altercations escalated into hospital visits. Eventually, it led to a fight that I will never forget. There is an old saying about mistreating animals, "If you beat or mistreat something long enough one of three things will happen:

1. The object will eventually submit to your demands.
2. The object will eventually turn against you.
3. The object will choose death over its current living conditions."

One day during one of our arguments, I decided it would be either him or me. I refused to let him control my life any longer. I wanted out and I did not care how it happened. I pushed him and pushed him to see how much nerve he really had. Midway through the argument I noticed he was carrying the gun.

"You're nothing but a child with a toy! You don't even have the guts to pull the trigger! Let me have it! I'll show you how to use it!" He walked over to me and slapped me with the back of his hand.

"How did that feel?" He asked me.

"How did what feel?" He slapped me, again. I noticed a lead crystal ashtray sitting on the tea table. It weighed at least three pounds. When he turned his back to walk away from me, I picked it up and threw it at him. The ashtray missed his head and hit him square in the back. Before I could blink, his hands were wrapped around my throat.

"Now what do you have to say for yourself smart mouth?" I looked into his eyes. I saw fear in his eyes. I was frightened he would pull the gun out. It was tucked in his pants. I struggled to get free. I could feel myself losing consciousness. "What are you gonna do now?" He tightened his grip around my throat. I could not speak. No sound would come out of my mouth. I continued to struggle with him. I finally connected a fist with his kidney. He let go screaming in pain.

"You should have killed me a long time ago! One of us will not make it out of this room alive tonight!" I saw a chance for me to get to the phone. I darted for it. He followed behind me screaming in my ear.

"Who are you calling, your family? They won't make it here in time to save your butt!" I could feel his hot breath against my neck. He grabbed my hair. I dialed 911. He threatened and cursed me. The operator could hear the commotion. She suggested I hang the phone up. She assured me the police were on their way. I reluctantly hung up. I pulled myself out of his grip and walked back into the living room. He followed closely behind me. "Who was that?"

"None of your business." I sat down on the couch. He sat across from me in a chair. He placed the gun on his lap. He was nervous. His foot was twitching uncontrollably. I became worried he would accidentally pull the trigger. I turned to face the patio door and watched the sheriff pull up. Anthony followed my glance.

"Well, they came quickly. You must be screwing one of them."

"Whatever you say. You know it all." Seconds before the police entered the apartment he threw the gun onto my lap. I moved my hands as far from the gun as I could. The officers came in without knocking. They came directly to me. One of them snatched the gun from my lap and asked who owned it. I pointed to my husband.

"What were you doing with the gun, ma'am?"

"My husband threw it into my lap before you entered the apartment."

"Do you realize, I can arrest you for possession of a fire arm within city limits?""How can you arrest me? I did not have the gun. He threatened me with it!" I stood up and faced the officer. I was angry. They were not going to dust it under the carpet any longer.

"Ma'am, sit down, please, before we have to restrain you."

"You better restrain me! One of us is not walking out of here alive." I sat back down on the couch. My husband started laughing. "You better get him out of my face!" The other officer took my husband outside to talk with him.

"What happened," the officer asked nonchalantly after my husband left the apartment.

I took a deep breath and explained to the officer what had happened. The officer looked at me like I was a hysterical maniac. The officer said nothing. I became distraught. I began to threaten them and my husband. The officer told me to calm down, but not this time. I refused to close the door this time. I refused to let all the emotions get buried this time. It was ending today, somehow. I had kept all my human emotions locked up in a safe place. I was ready for every last one of them to come to the surface.

Someone was going to pay this time. When I had seen the officer was not going to do anything, I slipped into silence. The other officer returned with my husband. The officers lectured us both on how violence was not the answer and that we needed counseling. I occasionally glanced and nodded as they talked pretending I was listening. Deep inside I was contemplating how I was going to kill my husband. They handed us both business cards for a counselor.

"I'll call first thing in the morning, sir." I looked at my husband. How pathetic. How are you going to call anyone if you are dead, I thought. The officers left after my husband showed them his registration for the gun. I sat down on the couch the rest of the day. I did not move or speak a word. I watched my husband intently as he went through the rest of the day like nothing ever happened. He eventually grew tired and went to bed. He shut the lights off leaving me in the dark.

There is no way for me to describe the way I felt at that point. I had a loathing hate for my husband. I did not even consider him human. He was sub-human to me. I had become such a good liar at hiding the truth that I knew no one would believe me, now. I knew it was too late to go running to my family to ask for the help I needed. I knew I had dug a hole and buried myself in it. I just needed a way to get out of it. I was afraid if I stayed where I was one of us would end up dead. Or worse, my son would end up hurt. I sat on the couch all night thinking. The night had slipped away before I knew it. I could hear Anthony moving around in the bedroom. I shuttered inside. I did not want him to touch me or speak to me. He finally peeped his head around the corner.

"What are you doing today?" I just looked at him. I did not let one word slip form my lips. "I guess you're not speaking today." He walked past me and went out the door. I sat where I was wondering what I was going to do. I knew I had to make my decision quickly. After a few minutes of taking inventory of my stuff and what I could pack and take with me, I made the decision to leave. The next day I found a good lawyer and filed for a divorce.

The next year and a half was one panic attack after another one. My husband refused to divorce me at first. He made it very difficult for me and said I was an abusive mother and that I had an adulterous affair while we were married. He had a detective monitoring every move I made. I could not go anywhere without it ending up before the judge in the courtroom. His futile attempts to scare me out of the divorce did not work. I determined to put him in my past. When Anthony finally realized I was not giving in to his petty tantrums, he agreed to the divorce upon one condition. He wanted all the abuse charges dropped. He made a plea with the judge that it would ruin his career. I only agreed to his terms to get the whole divorce over with.

I have heard a lot of men refer to their wives or girlfriends as their personal property. Their remarks sent shutters down my spine. I felt sorry for the person who was with them. Because of my first husband, I became overly aggressive toward men. I refused to be pushed around by anyone. I did not understand what real love was. I was not ready to enter into a new relationship, but I firmly believed I was able to go on with life without any type of help. I held my head up like a trooper, and walked right off the cliff.

CHAPTER THREE

"Because to every purpose there is time and judgement, therefore the misery of man is great upon him. For he knoweth not that which shall be: for who can tell him when it shall be?"

Ecclesiastes 8:6,7

****

A boy worked as an apprentice for a butcher. Everyday the boy eagerly watched the butcher. He grew in knowledge and skill. The boy became very good at is work. The boy knew with a lot of hard work, he would be able to run the store on his own. The butcher said that he still needed to learn more about the business, but the boy was willing to learn. One day the butcher received a large order of whole chickens. The butcher was very busy and could not see after his order. The boy, wanting to please the butcher, volunteered to unload and sign for the order.

"Separate the chickens from the crates and put them in the freezer," the butcher yelled as the boy ran into the back of the store. In his haste, the boy did not hear the butcher. The boy counted the order and signed for it like he was taught. He walked back up to the front of the store to see if the butcher was still busy. The butcher was still taking care of several customers. The boy retreated to the back of the store and began to take the chickens out of the crates.

After a few hours went by, the butcher began to wonder what was taking the boy so long. The butcher went to the back of the store. He noticed the boy by the freezer. The butcher slowly walked toward him.

"Look, I've cut up five crates of chickens. I wanted to get a jump start on them since you were so busy." The boy was delighted over the work he had done.

"This is not what I told you to do. I told you to separate the chickens and put them in the freezer. I did not tell you to cut them up." The butcher was upset, but was able to stay calm.

"How can I make amends," the boy asked sincerely?

"You can't. The people who ordered the chickens will be here to pick them up in a few hours." The butcher walked back to the front of the store shutting the door between them.

Every one of us is brought into the kingdom of God for a purpose. God waits patiently for us to get to the place we need to be in order for us to fulfill his perfect will for our lives. It is up to us to grow in knowledge and wisdom to make ourselves ready for God.

> *"Study to show thyself approved unto God,*
> *A workman that needeth not be ashamed,*
> *Rightly dividing the word of truth."*

2 Timothy 2:15

We also need to learn to hear the voice of God. We must stop what we are doing, listen to his voice and comprehend what is said in order to do God's perfect will.

"And thine ears shall hear a word behind thee,
Saying, this is the way, walk ye in it,
When ye turn to the right hand,
And turn to the left."

Isaiah 30:21

Some of us are in such a hurry to do what we feel God wants us to do; we fail to listen to his direction.

"For he beholdeth himself, and goeth his way,
And straightway forgeteth what manner of man he was."

James 1:24

When it is time for us to give an account to God, we will profess all the good works we feel we have for him. If we have not done his perfect will, he will in turn say:

"Not every one that sayeth unto me,
Lord, Lord, shall enter into the Kingdom of Heaven;
But he that doeth the will of my Father which is in Heaven.
Many will say to me in that day,
Lord, Lord have we not prophesied in thy name?
And in thy name have cast out devils?
And in thy name done many wonderful works?
And then will I profess to them,
I never knew you: depart from me,
Ye that work iniquity."

Mathew 7:21-23

Are you performing God's perfect will or what you believe he wants you to do?

****

If you have been around horses, you know that they are not very intelligent animals. A horse will literally let itself get burned up in a fire. The horse becomes so terrified it stands still until someone attempts to lead it out of the fire. In order to do this, the rescuer blinds the horse by covering up the eyes of the horse. The horse will then peacefully follow as it is being guided through the fire. We as children of God do the same thing. We become so frightened by the tactics of the devil we stand still and do not go forward. We let the fire lap at our bodies slowly killing us spiritually. One of two things will happen. We will either call out for help or just stand there and burn. Calling out for help enables God to come and rescue us. God will put blinders on us. God teaches us to walk by faith not sight. If we look at our physical surroundings, we become frightened and stay where we feel comfortable regardless of if we will die spiritually for it or not. If we walk by faith and trust God for his protection, God will always lead us out of the fire no matter how bad it becomes.

I had survived an abusive relationship. Instead of checking my inventory to see what was missing, I jumped right into another relationship. I was not ready. I did not believe I needed any time to heal. I could not understand that people need to adjust from one situation to the other. I guess I was so use to being in a bad relationship, that I thought a good one would be easy to handle. A friend of mine had told me once; "If you have been with someone a certain amount of time it will take an equal amount of time to work out all the emotions affiliated with that relationship." I have never been alone long enough to see if it works. I have always gone from one relationship to the next.

Keith was an easy person to fall in love with. He was so much different than Anthony. We grew close quickly. We spent almost every day together. I lived with my grandparents. They continued to watch my son while I worked and went to school. They began to get angry because I was not home enough. I did not care. I wanted to start my life over and the faster the better. My grandmother constantly asked where I was going. So to avoid her asking me the question, I stayed away from the house even more. I tried to involve my son in some of my activities, but I was questioned so much that I would just leave him at the house.

I believed I was in love with Keith and lived like I was. I still refused to listen to the voice of reason. I acted like a person with blinders on. I only saw what was in front of me. I had changed. I grew further and further from anyone who honestly loved me. I did not want that kind of love. It meant responsibility. It meant commitment. I wanted to be able to leave anytime. I wanted no strings attached. My anger threshold was low and I often took the offensive if anyone showed any kind of opposition toward me. I think the most dangerous attitude I had was I knowing I was an adult and could do what ever I wanted without any questions. I feel guilty for a great deal of things I have done to people. I lived for me only. Everyone else had to take care of his or her own self. The people I had in my life served their purposes at the time. The people I thought I loved only filled any empty gap that existed in my life. They were only the patches not the solution.

Keith was romantic. He was a person that deserved more than what I was giving him. His heart was genuine. I thought mine was at the time. He sent flowers, cards, and balloons to my job. My fellow workers became jealous. Keith was spoiling me. I enjoyed every bit of it. I let down old guards that I had put up. I felt closer to Keith than I had to anyone in a long time. Keith was not without his problems, either. His father had died of cancer his senior year of high school and he never graduated high school. His mother and I both tried to get him to finish his GED, but he held on to the contention that he did not need a degree to get a good job. He assumed he would get hired in a high paying position without any difficulty. He would not settle for just a good job until he was promoted. He wanted the promotion to come before he got the job. This angered me and we fought often over it.

I had a lot of issues of my own that were in need of repair. I had incurred a great amount of debt from my first marriage. I was having difficulties paying it off. I hated for Fridays to come. I knew whatever money I had was already spent. I became very distressed over it, but it still did not curve my spending habits. Even today I could not understand why I would spend money I did not have. It seemed the more I had the more in debt I became. I saw no feasible solution in sight. I did not want to lose the good credit rating I had. I worked hard to pay my bills on time. I began looking for a second job to take the heavy load off my shoulders.

I know the stress I had been in for the past four years had taken its toll on my health. My health slowly took a turn for the worse. I was seeing my doctor on a weekly basis. She finally tested me for cancer, arthritis, lupus, and thyroid problems. The lupus test, the arthritis tests, and the thyroid tests came back with results I did not want to hear. I thank God the cancer results came back negative. However, I did have arthritis and thyroid disease. The lupus test came back too close to make an objective diagnosis. The doctor explained that I would need to be tested every year for lupus. It frightened me at first, but I became more interested in the prescriptions she was about to write out. I saw my salvation in the palm of her hands. She handed me the tickets I needed to take away more than the physical pain I had developed over the past few years.

I became slowly addicted to prescription drugs. I would take pain pills to calm down so I could sleep. No one suspected anything. I was twenty-one years old and felt like I had lived my entire life already. I was not worried about the future. I did not even think I would live to be thirty years of age. I just lived for the day that was at hand. I had taking the pills down to a fine art. I knew how many milligrams it took for me to overdose according to my body weight. I often came close to these levels. At times I would sleep entire days away. It frightens me, today, to think how my entire family could not see the changes that were taking place with me.

I know the drugs were having an adverse affect on my behavior. I blamed everything on everyone, but myself. Keith and I were arguing a lot more often. At first, it started as yelling back and forth. It developed into physical contact. I was more aggressive toward Keith. I became physical with him before he had the chance to touch me. I actually believed I was doing the right thing. I believed I was defending myself. The fact was that I had become an abuser. I could not see it at the time. It was a long time before I could even admit to anyone what I had become.

Despite our arguing, Keith and I got married. We were married in a courthouse with close friends and relatives. After the wedding we had a small reception. I chose to live near my grandparents so I could see my son more often. That did not happen. I became even more involved with my job and school. These things became my excuse for not spending time with anyone. Soon after we were married Keith became unemployed. I was faced with paying bills I could not afford alone. I took a second job. Sleep deprivation led me to experiment with amphetamines. I was surviving off mere pills alone. The arguing became more volatile. Keith never could understand my outbursts. I felt like a ravenous animal at times. I could not even control myself. It was almost like I was watching myself form a distance.

The last thing I could have imagined happened. My grandmother on my father's side died suddenly in her sleep. My grandmother and I had just started a relationship a few years earlier. Her death took a toll on me. I felt robbed. I was just getting to know her. The most upsetting thing was my husband. He just wanted a trip to California. He had always wanted to live in California. I did not even want him to go. I wanted to be alone, but Keith persisted on going with me. I made arrangements to drive. I thought it would be more cost effective than flying. My father wired me some money to make the trip.

We left early the Saturday morning. It was January and we chose to take the southern route to California. The northern route would have been almost impossible to drive due to the mountain regions being covered in snow and ice. Keith drove from Ohio to Tennessee. I drove from Tennessee to Texas. Keith took over and drove through the panhandle of Texas. When we arrived in New Mexico, it was 70 degrees. By the time we reached Gallup, New Mexico, it was 20 degrees with two feet of snow that fell in only one hour. The roads were covered in a foot of ice. Keith was too frightened to drive. I was exhausted, but drove anyway. I knew we had to make it to California by Monday. We had no time to waste. We became stranded on the highway along with other travelers for two hours in one spot. I managed to drive through Arizona. I was fatigued and could no longer drive. Keith happily took over when he realized we were at the border of California. I was angry, but too tired to argue with him. I let him drive the rest of the way to my father's house.

We arrived at my father's house Monday morning only a few hours before the funeral. We hurriedly got dressed and headed out to the funeral. I had no chance to rest. My grandmother was cremated a few days earlier. The funeral services were held in a reception room in the apartment building she lived in. They were more like a memorial service. I saw family I had not seen since I was a very small child. It felt strange to see them. They were strangers to me. They were, however, happy to see me. Keith was enjoying the whole experience. He quickly made himself feel at home. I felt he had no right to include himself in my family's activities. I could feel hate growing inside of me toward him.

I had seen my father a year earlier when he had visited Ohio. I had thought the hate and bitterness he had toward my mother would have died down since then. My father openly expressed his contempt for my mother. I listened to him nodding every so often. It amazed me how much hate he had for her. I listened until I had had enough. I exploded. I told my father every bad memory I had of him. He said nothing. He could not believe I remembered everything that had happened when I was a small child. He accused my mother of telling the stories to me. I expressed to him vividly that my mother never told me anything about him. I explained to him that my memories were just that. They were memories. Still in disbelief, he interrogated me. Once he saw that I knew exact details, he finally believed they were memories and not stories told to me. He also felt ashamed of it. He knew I had remembered every little detail. I remembered the drug use and his extramarital affair with my stepmother. He stared at me for a long time before speaking again.

"I always knew there was something special about you."

"What do you mean?" I wanted to know. I had always felt something better was out there for me and wanted the secret to unlocking the door. I had hoped my father had the key.

"I can't tell you. You will find out in due time. It's not time right now." I wanted to slap my father. I brushed off what he had said on the surface, but deep down I knew he was right. I had felt something tug on me for a long time. I just did not know what it was.

Keith and I stayed in California a week. We left early Friday morning. Keith wanted to see Las Vegas and had suggested going there on the way home. I wanted to see Las Vegas at least one time, also. So, I agreed. It wound up becoming a mistake on my part. At the time, I was not aware Keith had a gambling problem. He kept it a secret from me. We allotted a small amount of money to gamble with. It was a matter of only a few short hours before it was gone. I had my fun and was ready to go home. Keith was not.

"Pull some money out of the account. I promise I can recoup everything we've lost."

"No, we don't have anymore money to gamble with!" I was furious.

"It's my money!" He sounded like a child crying over a toy.

"Excuse me. How is it your money? That money is for your car payment!"

"I promise I'll double the money. Just let me have it!" Just to prove him wrong, I gave him the money. I went to the car and sat in it. I pulled out of the parking lot a few times to leave him. I just could not do it. It had been only two hours when he returned to the car empty handed. He got into the car with a solemn look on his face. I knew he lost all of the money. I started the car and left the parking lot. I was boiling inside. When I reached the out skirts of Las Vegas, I could not hold it in any longer. I had to say something.

"You lost all the money didn't you?" I looked over at him. He was staring out the window. "You can't ignore me forever! We still have fifteen hundred miles to drive! Quite honestly, I prefer you walk home!"

"You always got to run your mouth! Don't you ever shut up?" He leaned his seat back to go to sleep.

"You see, I have this problem, I feel I am obligated to tell someone when they are acting like a idiot! Oh, by the way, if I can't sleep, you're not sleeping!"

"Stop me," he yelled. I slammed on the brakes. He flew into the dashboard of the car. As he got up from the floor his fist connected with my leg. I put the car in park. We were in the middle of the road. I refused to go anywhere.

"You just made a mistake."

"Yeh, marrying you!" He finally got situated back in his seat.

"Don't you ever touch me, again. I will take you off this planet!" I threw a punch that landed on his chest.

"Anything would be better than being here with you!" He put his seat belt on.

"You won't need that!"

"Why?" He asked.

"Because you're not staying in this car, that's why!"

"Oh, and what are you going to do? I'm not getting out!" I pulled the car off the road. I shut the car off and took the keys out of the ignition. I got out and walked over to the passenger's side of the car. I opened the door and tried to drag him out of the car. He fought back, but could not do much. His seat belt was still buckled.

"Oooh, I'm so tired of your lazy butt!" I slammed the car door shut and walked to the rear of the car. I stayed there for a few minutes to calm down. When I was ready, I got back into the car. "When we get home, you need to find a place to live. I can't be with someone like you any longer."

"What about you? I don't know how any man can stand being with you!" Both of us remained silent the majority of the way home. We arrived home Sunday afternoon. It had recently snowed in Ohio, but we missed the worst part. I was relieved we were home.

There were several messages on the answering machine. I was surprised to received one from a job I had applied for. I had applied to work in a new prison a few months earlier. They had told me they could not hire me, because I was not able to go to the training. Apparently, they were able to work it out that I would only need to go to training for thirty hours. My past military experience and the college courses I had completed were enough to satisfy the state's criteria. I knew this would be my chance to save money in order for me to leave Keith.

Keith was still unemployed. I decided that it would be easier for me to go ahead and find a cheaper apartment to live in. After a few days I found one I liked. We both moved in February 1st. It was a small apartment. It was almost impossible to get all our stuff into it. Moving into the apartment helped the financial problems slightly, but it was not enough. I decided, after much thought, I needed to file for bankruptcy. I had Keith's car reposed. He was upset about it, but I did not care. I was the one paying for it. I took precautions with the checking accounts. I took his name off every one of them.

I warned him on several occasions that the marriage was over. I stopped buying household items like food. He increasingly grew even angrier with me. The fights became more violent. On occasion he would call the police on me, but it did not bother me. From past experience, I knew how they would respond. Keith knew he was just as responsible as I was for the fall of the entire relationship. The last possible thing I would have imagined him doing, he did. During a heated argument, Keith pushed over my granddaughter's clock my grandfather had made by hand. I stood and stared at it for a few seconds. Keith backed up away from me. I looked at him. Tears had begun to fall down my cheeks. I wanted to kill him. I think he knew it. He continued to back away form me. I grabbed the first thing I could get my hands on and knocked him down to the ground. As he tried to get up, I kicked him in the back. I grabbed my purse and left for the night. The next day I applied for another apartment in the same complex. A week later I moved into it.

I told my family I was applying for a divorce. I expected them to tell me not to do it, but they said nothing. I could tell they were concerned. This would be my second divorce. I was only twenty-two years old. My grandmother occasionally asked me why. I just told her I was not happy. I told Keith that he was going to pay for the divorce. I refused to spend any money on anything connected with him. He refused to file. I had run into an old high school friend that I dated casually while we were in high school. We began dating again. He knew I had recently left my husband, but he did not know we were still married. He just assumed the divorce had gone through. He was deep into the occult and sparked my interest in it again.

I loved my new apartment and my newfound freedom, but barely had the time to enjoy it. I was working a forty-hour job, going to school full-time and working three days a week at the prison. I was only getting two to three hours of sleep a day. I was beginning to feel it. I was falling asleep in school and my grades were starting to drop. My health was getting worse, but I did not stop pushing myself. I continued with school and both my jobs. I thought I was happy. I was on my own. I was proving to myself I did not need to be with someone in order to survive.

I never truly realized how bad of shape I was in until recently. My health was declining and my mental capacities were failing, also. I was headed for a complete mental and physical breakdown. Sometimes I wonder if I was trying to commit suicide. I could not intentionally do it on my own. Something deep down inside of me kept telling me to hang on. There was a yearning deep down to see the future that was promised to me. I knew there was something more than what was happening at that present moment. It is a hard feeling to explain, but I believe it is what kept me fighting to go on. It gave me strength when I had none, and brought me encouragement when I needed it. I would have sworn to a priest that I was not in bad shape with God. At the time I did not know it was God's love that protected me. It was God's grace that let me live my life without one single thought toward the God that put breath in my lungs. It was God's mercies that did not wipe me off the face of the earth. God had plans for me regardless of how much I wanted to end my own life. In Jeremiah, chapter 1, verse 5, God told Jeremiah; "Before I formed thee in the belly I knew thee; and before thou camest forth out of the womb I sanctified thee…"

Despite God's knowledge of our activities and despite the lack of integrity and moral character that affects ninety percent of the population, God still loves us. He loves us in our lowest state and he loves us in our highest state. The times we go through are for a short while. We must believe God's promises. We must continue without hesitation. Hesitating causes death both physical and spiritual. We may not understand what we are going through. We may not want to take the first step, but we must not fight it, either. I think deep down we all hear God's call for us. We feel that inner longing to be loved unconditionally, and only God can fill that desire.

CHAPTER FOUR

"Thou broughtest us into the net; thou laidest affliction upon our loins.
Thou hast caused men to ride over our heads;
We went through fire and through water:
But thou broughtest us out into a wealthy place."

Psalm 66:11,12

****

A young woman returned home late from work. Upon arriving at her house, she noticed all the lights were on and the front door was wide open. Too frightened to pull into her own driveway, she pulled into her neighbor's. Watching her house, she fumbled through her purse for her cellular phone. She felt relieved when she could finally feel the phone in her hand. The young woman pulled the phone out and dialed 911. The phone beeped loudly in her ear letting her know the battery was too low to place the call. A deep sense of fear overcame her. She sat for a few minutes wondering what she was going to do. All of a sudden she realized she could use her neighbor's phone. She cautiously got out of her car and ran for her neighbor's front door. She rang the doorbell. She waited a few seconds and rang the doorbell again. The young woman noticed a light come on inside of the house.

"Who is it," a voice called from inside?

"It's your neighbor, Loretta." The young woman answered occasionally looking back at her home.

"Loretta," the voice paused. "I don't know any Loretta."

"I'm your neighbor. I've lived next to you for five years." The young woman grew anxious.

"Sorry, I don't know you." The light inside of the home went off.

"No, please help me." The young woman whispered back in tears. She turned and looked back at her house in utter fear.

Communication is a key factor in any relationship. It can make or break a relationship. Without communication a relationship will fizzle into nothing. The same is true with God. We must keep our communication lines open with Him in prayer.

"Thou shalt make thy prayer unto him and he shall hear thee…"

Job 22:27

A relationship takes commitment and hard work. A relationship with God requires the same. Unlike a relationship with an individual that has no promises, God promises to meet us halfway.

"Draw nigh to God and he will draw nigh to you…"

James 4:8

When we have a relationship with someone, they are more likely to help us in a time of need. When we have a relationship with God, he will always help us.

"I sought the Lord, and he heard me, and delivered me from all my fears."

Psalm 34:4

God promises that he will always be with us, but just like any other relationship if you forsake the one you love, they will forsake you. God is no different.

"...the Lord is with you while ye be with him;
And if ye seek him, he will be found of you;
But if ye forsake him, he will forsake you."

2 Chronicles 15:2

Do you have a relationship with God?

****

After the initial shock of two failed marriages slowly passed away, I was faced with an unknown world. I did not know what to do. My health was deteriorating. The stress and lack of sleep continued to control me. I refused to slow down. I was only twenty-two. I was young. I believed my body could handle the torture I was putting it through. My pill popping became worse. I was addicted. My body craved them. I craved them. At times, I would accidentally overdose. I normally ended up in the hospital with a migraine headache. The doctors never questioned me. They gave me more drugs at the hospital so I could sleep it off. They kept me there to monitor my condition until they felt I could go home. At the time I never thought how much danger I was in when I received those shots. At the time, I could have cared less. I could have easily died, slipped into a coma or I could have had some sort of brain damage.

I enjoyed being on my own even though I never had any time to myself. I was either at work, school, or the bars. My family continued to take care of my son. I was in no shape to take care of myself. It was rare that I saw them or my son. My grandmother asked me to move back with them a few times, but I did not want to. I guess she thought she could protect me if I were under her roof. I wanted more freedom than they were willing to offer. I had grown use to being on my own and making my own decisions. I did not want them to find out who I really was. I did not want to face them or their questions.

I continued dating my friend from high school. We were growing closer. I still guarded my feelings. He did not make me any promises, and I did not want to catch myself in another dead end relationship. I would learn years down the road that my real problem in any relationship I was ever in was my lack of patience. I would become tired of waiting and either forced the relationship or ended it. The norm was for me to end it with a good man and begin another relationship with a bad man. This relationship was no different. My friend was a good man. He treated me well. My problem was he made no promises. It was not long before I messed it up.

A man from my second job became interested in me. At first I did not give in to his constant flattery. I felt he was putting up a front, but a month later I gave in. We made arrangements to go on a date. I was vulnerable and he offered more attention than my friend I was dating at the time. It did not matter to me that he was of another race. I had never dated anyone from another race and did not know what to expect. I let my guard down to quickly. He consumed my life. He was not a bad person. He was just young and immature. It was not long, however, I found out he was cheating on me with another woman. Actually, I should say a young girl. I confronted him and the girl. He denied it. I made the mistake to stay with him.

As the news got out I was dating a black man, I found out who were my real friends and who were not. A few stuck around, but they could not understand why I was dating out of my race. Others resisted the relationship. They dealt with it by making derogatory remarks toward me. My family was instantly against the relationship. I was told not to bring him around. It hurt my feelings that my family was even like that. I had believed they were more excepting. From childhood to adulthood, I never heard them speak any wrong toward any race. They became more protective of my son. I stopped asking to see him altogether. I guess that is why I clung so desperately to Marquis.

I knew Marquis was still seeing other woman. I refused to leave him. I suffered scrutiny and scorn from too many people to give up on the relationship. I believed I was the one doing something wrong. I did everything I could to satisfy him, but it did not work. I was driving myself crazy trying to please him. I became hysterical when his appreciation was not shown. I encouraged his behavior even more when I would let him borrow my car. I figured if he had a car it would not give him any excuses to stay gone all night long. He would have to return to the house in time for me to go to work. That is exactly what he did. He returned just in time for me to leave for work.

My demons from the past constantly harassed me. I grew angrier toward the world. Hate was my drive for survival. There was nothing else in me. I became an empty shell. So when I began inflicting injury on myself, I did not associate it with having a problem. All I knew was pain. Being without pain was strange to me. I was only doing what I knew of life. Life was full of pain and I had to inflict it to feel I was alive. No one, like anything else I did, ever caught on. I kept it a secret. I was good at explaining the injuries away. I was taking forensics and investigation courses in college. I knew exactly what it took to receive any kind of injury. I would carefully work out the details before I went to the hospital if the injury was bad enough. My choice weapons were knives, hammers, and razor blades. I would have liked to tell everyone that I was using drugs or alcohol when I inflicted the injuries, but I was not. I was always perfectly sober. I was desperately crying for someone to release me from the prison I was locked up in, but no one saw through the brick walls I had built up.

It amazes me how much I let the devil influence me when I was in the world. To even try to understand why anyone would ever take a knife to his or her own flesh and cut his or her own flesh is unimaginable to me. I still cannot fathom it. I have a scar on my arm from a knife wound I inflicted on myself only a few years ago. I had lied to the doctor and told him I had to pull my dog from a pile of railroad ties. I explained that there was glass in with the wood that I did not see. The glass cut my arm. The wound was over seven inches long with jagged edges. It was in need of stitches and I was warned it would leave a nasty scar. The doctor, who was an animal lover, performed plastic surgery on my arm for free for saving my dog. The scar is a reminder to me everyday of the place I had come from.

There is not one day I do not thank Jesus for my life. Jesus kept me a live when I did not even want to be a live. The devil was trying to check me out of the world, but a stronger force would not let him. Now, when I look back, I can see the demons sitting next to me encouraging me to do whatever it took to end my life. It is a scary thing to be in the position I was in and live to tell about it. I know with assurance I should be dead. Who, but God, could love someone whom did not love her own self? Who, but God, would have allowed that very same person to survive these experiences and still have their full mental capacity? God had given me the spirit of survival. I was a fighter. I just did not know for what.

At this point in my life, my behavior was obviously very destructive. I did not know how to deal with all the hate and anger that took refuge inside of me. I had built a fortress around myself just like the devil wanted. I was alone right where he wanted me. I knew the things I was doing were wrong. I just could not admit it. Admitting I was wrong would have meant becoming an even bigger disappointment to my family. It would, also, mean I was a failure in my very own eyes. I tucked

anything and everything into the back of my mind. I made myself
believe I could deal with it at a later time. My behavior was erratic. I
went into rages of anger over simple matters. I had no common respect
for anyone.

Without a second income, I decided I needed to move to save money.
The place I chose was not the best, but it was cheap. It was on the west
side of town in the city. This was going to be a new experience for me.
The last time I lived in the city limits I was three years old. Marquis was
still being unfaithful to me. I would go into a fit of rage anytime I found
out about his lack of commitment. The fights became physical. A lot of
times he would grow tired of me and leave for the day. This, of course,
would increase my anger toward him. I spent many nights crying wondering where Marquis was. I fell deeper and deeper into depression. I
wanted to leave him, but I could not. I lost my family over him and I
was going to make the relationship work just to prove them wrong.

Marquis' friend, Devon, his girlfriend, Rebecca, and I hung out
together. Rebecca and I spent many nights on the phone trying to see if
one or the other knew where Marquis and Devon were. We basically
used each other to keep up with Marquis and Devon. We were friends
on the surface. Each of us kept information from the other. We knew
what the other's boyfriend was doing. I could not afford to become
close with anyone. I did not want that stigma in my life. Yes, I did think
I loved Marquis, but now that I know what true love is, I know I really
did not love him. Marquis filled in a void. He filled the void temporarily
like Anthony and Keith did previously. I get sick every time I think of all
the years I have let pass with no accomplishments to remember them
by.

After Marquis and I were in our apartment for a month or two, we
found out that Rebecca and Devon were going to be evicted. Rebecca
had just found out she was pregnant and I felt sorry for her. I knew it
would be hard for her. Out of whatever kindness I still had left in me, I
said she and Devon could move in with Marquis and I. In a small way, I

was happy Marquis' friend was staying with us. Now, Marquis did not have as many excuses to leave. However, after a month I was tired of everybody. I wanted everybody to leave. Rebecca and Devon were having problems and she needed a friend. I had my own problems and could not deal with someone else's. I was not equipped to be the friend she needed. I just said things to appease her and went on my way.

The last thing I expected was for me to become pregnant. I went to the hospital feeling a little ill. I was drinking heavily the month before, and had quit using a lot of the pills I had become accustomed to. I thought my body was going through withdrawal symptoms. When the doctor came in and told me I was pregnant, she thought something else was wrong. She asked if I needed to see a counselor. I refused and asked if I could leave. I left and went home. Marquis had found out another girl he was dating had become pregnant. I did not know what to expect him to do after I told him. My mind was full of thoughts as I drove the short distance back to the apartment. I worried about my family's reaction. I worried about his family's reaction. I worried about my reaction. I was in no shape to be a mother. Only the month before I was popping pills and drinking. I finally reached the apartment and went up the long high stairwell to tell Marquis.

Marquis and Devon did not go to work that day. I pulled Marquis to the side and told him I was pregnant. I expected him to be happy, but he just looked at me blankly. He was the one to break the news to Rebecca and Devon. They looked at me the same way. They knew of the other girl that was pregnant. Rebecca broke the ice a little bit and congratulated me. I smiled, but deep inside I was crying. I did not know how my family would react or how I was going to get through a pregnancy by myself. I knew I would have no help. What I did not know was how dangerously close I would come to losing my baby.

After a few weeks, I got news that the other girl that Marquis had gotten pregnant had lost her baby. I was relieved, but I knew he would not stop cheating on me. I decided it was best for me just to seclude myself from everyone. I stayed away from my family as much as possible. I only visited them if I had to. I wound up telling my mom I was pregnant only two months before I was due. She was highly upset. I believe it hurt her more that I did not tell her sooner than me having a bi-racial child. My grandmother was just plain upset. The fact I was not married made her even more livid. I was very slender from being sick. I did not even look like I was pregnant. A lot of people kept telling Marquis that I was faking it. Marquis knew I was pregnant. He also knew the reason why I did not look pregnant. More times than none there was no food in the house. I would go days without eating. Marquis did not contribute to any of the bills. I had to feed us, pay the rent and utilities on my salary. He did whatever he chose to with the money he earned.

I began bleeding in my third month. I bled throughout my entire pregnancy. The doctor noticed that my placenta was becoming unattached from my uterus wall, also. I was afraid for my unborn child, but I took it casually. I was to stop all strenuous activity, but I could not. I had to take care of the house, Marquis, Devon, Rebecca, and myself. Rebecca used the excuse she was pregnant and tired. Devon was just plain lazy and Marquis did not believe he had to do anything. This was the norm. I became their slave. They knew I could not stand for the house to be dirty and I would clean up after them. It was something I should have never started with them. By March my doctor put me on bed rest. It was always the last thing on my list to do.

I had grown tired of the place I was currently living and wanted to move. After only a few days of searching, I found a house on the east side of town. Everyone was against the move. I did not listen to them. I was weary of their opinions. It amazed me how opinionated people became when they were not doing anything about their own situations. I was concerned about me at this point. They did not matter too much to me. My grandfather helped me move. It surprised me Marquis even helped. Devon had returned to prison for parole violation and Rebecca relied on some friends to help her move. Rebecca moved in with her friends. I guess she knew how upset I had gotten over the entire situation. It took me three weeks to unpack everything. Marquis did not help with this step of the moving. I hauled mattresses, dressers and various other things up two flights of stairs. Marquis kept promising he would help, but I knew it would never come.

I was alone in the house most of the time. It was a big old house that made a lot of noise. I spent quite a few nights staying awake and listening to the creaks and groaning the house made. It did not help that it was located in a bad neighborhood either. I visited Rebecca quite a lot. I was becoming bored of not working. I felt I was going to go stir crazy. On one occasion when I visited Rebecca, she asked me to take her somewhere. I could tell something was wrong. After we got into the car, she started talking to me.

"Jennifer, I really need to leave here, but I have no where to go." She paused for a little bit. I listened to her steadily watching the road ahead of me. I showed her no expression. "She has three cats, two dogs and a ferret. I can't stay there any longer. The house stinks. There's roaches everywhere." I heard the plea in her voice. I could feel a yearning for companionship scream from inside of me. Marquis was not fulfilling his role as a friend. After much thought, I answered her.

"Rebecca, I don't mind you moving back in with Marquis and I. There is one thing, though. You got to help me with the house. I know you are by yourself, but I still need you to help. I am supposed to be on bed rest." I could see a smile appear on her face.

"Thank you." I could tell she was relieved. A feeling of regret came over me. Inside, I told myself I was too kind. Sooner or later, I knew I would regret letting her move in with Marquis and I.

I had given Marquis money for a down payment for a car. It was really to keep him from borrowing mine. My grandfather had helped me get a car and I did not want Marquis to tear it up. This was Marquis' ticket to stay gone. I often asked him if he was cheating on me again. He kept telling me it was my imagination. I knew better. I found girls' phone numbers in his clothing. Some of them were bold enough to come to the house. I confronted them without hesitation, of course. It was my job to keep up with what was going on. Some of them were more cordial than others. I was oblivious to self- preservation. I wanted one of them to touch me. I wanted to vent my anger and frustrations on them. It never happened. Some became aggressive, but they never laid a hand on me.

During one of my routine ultrasounds, I found out I was having a boy. I desperately wanted a girl. The news upset me some. I figured Marquis would be happy. After my doctor's appointment, I called him at work. At first he did not want to know, but then he gave in. He was thrilled he was having a little boy. He could tell I was upset. He knew I wanted a girl.

"Maybe one of these days you'll get to have a girl." His voice was calm.

"Maybe," I said in return.

"Well, I need to get back to work. I'll see you in a little bit."

"All right, bye" I hung up the pay phone and walked back to the car. Some tears clouded my eyes. Rebecca was in the car waiting. She looked at me. At first she did not say anything, but she finally asked what was wrong.

"Are you alright?"

"I'm fine."

"Marquis wasn't upset you were having a boy was he?" I could hear her voice lower into her throat.

"No, he was happy. I'm upset I'm having a boy."

"Why?"

"I just wanted to have a girl for my second child."

"Well, maybe the ultrasound is wrong and you'll have a girl."

"Not my luck," I answered her.

By the middle of May I was ready to return to work. I could not stand sitting at the house any longer. I was going crazy. I was bored and the pregnancy seemed like it was going to last for an eternity. I convinced my doctor to let me go back to work. With much hesitation, he finally agreed. Work was someplace I did not want to be either, but it was better than sitting at the house. At least the day went by faster. Everything went fine the first few weeks. My stress level steadily rose. I had a stressful job and was taking everything personal like most pregnant women do. A few of the customers knew I was having a problem pregnancy and tried to lay off of me a little bit. Their kindness just resulted in my supervisor getting mad because he was receiving my calls. I explained I was not responsible for what the customers did. He was having problems of his own and sympathized with me.

The first week of June Rebecca had her baby. I stayed with her all night until the next morning when she finally delivered her baby. She had a little girl. I was a little jealous. I became depressed and went home exhausted. I called off work and slept all day. A few days later her boyfriend was released from prison. The beginning of troubles I never thought I would have to deal with started that day. Everything was going smoothly for a little while. Then I began to notice something going on. I could smell something strange burning in the house at night after I went to bed. I had never smelled crack being smoked before and did not know what it was at first. I just ignored it for as long as I could, but I was forced to face reality the day Rebecca was arrested for solicitation and I knew the reason she was soliciting. She had started using crack again. She called me and begged me to believe she had not done anything. I was not falling for their tricks and games any longer. A few days later, she returned to the house. She continued to try and convince me she had not done anything. I blew up at everyone. Rebecca and Devon left me alone as much as possible.

I never fully recovered from the exhaustion of staying up all night with Rebecca the night she had her baby. I started to call off work a few times a week. My doctor finally pulled me out of work, again. He grew tired of writing excuses for my supervisor. My stress test was off the charts. My doctor insisted I rest. I could not do that. I had to watch the house day and night. I had things stolen. People I did not know came in and out of my house all through the night. I complained to Marquis constantly. He confronted Rebecca and Devon, but it never worked. Marquis made an effort to stay at the house more often. I often wondered if he was involved in their activity, also. He just did not seem to care too much about their activities.

Rebecca and Devon's drug habit became increasingly worse. They would leave for hours at a time leaving their daughter in their room by herself. I often went up to check on her. Their room was always filled with a thick cloud of smoke from the crack. The smell of it made me sick. I became worried enough of it would enter my system and harm my son. I stopped checking on their daughter. Marquis began retrieving their daughter and bringing her into our room. Sometimes we wondered how long it would take for them to realize their daughter was gone. An hour, or more later, Rebecca would knock on our door looking for her child. Marquis got out of bed and took the baby to Rebecca. A few times he gave her a lecture about leaving the baby alone. She would just look at him and say it was her child and she could do whatever she wanted. I threatened to call child protective services, but became afraid they would take my son when he was born. I felt like a prisoner in my own home.

I was three weeks late when I finally went into labor. Marquis surprised me and stayed with me the whole time. I dilated quickly, but my labor was not producing any results. Despite the problems I was having, I managed to deliver my second son naturally. They preformed a numerous amount of tests on him to make sure he was healthy. They were worried that the problems I was having while I was pregnant would adversely affect my son. The tests showed he was healthy. I was thrilled. I knew I would not be able to handle a sick baby with everything that was going on at my house. I took the time I was at the hospital to rest. I knew me not being at the house was an invitation for disaster, but I did not care. As long as I did not know about it, I did not care.

I was anxious about going home. I almost did not want to go. I knew the house would be in a shambles. I knew no one took care of anything. I, also, knew that the confusion would send me even deeper into depression. I had stopped using pills and drinking alcohol during my pregnancy. I knew if I stayed in the same environment, I would begin using. I could not admit to myself I was an addict. I was an intelligent educated person. People like me were not addicts. People like me were too intelligent to become an addict. We knew when to stop. We knew when to say no. That was the very same attitude kept me in the dark for years. I felt I was above everyone else that had an addiction problem. I figured the expensive alcohol and prescription drugs were in a totally different category than heroin, crack or marijuana.

The day I went home Marquis and I were in a car accident. Marquis did not buckle my son's car seat into the car. Of course his car seat flew forward. I managed to stop it before he hit the dashboard. My heart had jumped into my throat. My adrenaline was on over kill.

"You idiot," I screamed! "You said the car seat was buckled into the car! What are you trying to do, kill your son?" I was furious. I could not contain my anger. Marquis got out of the car to check to see if there was any damage to the other car. The owner of the other car got out and seen my son and I sitting in the car. He immediately came over and asked if we were hurt. He told Marquis that there was no damage and not to worry about it. Marquis got back in the car.

"He said not to worry about it. So I'm not." Marquis put the car in gear and drove off. He looked at me and smiled. He knew I was upset.

"Screw you!" I was too upset to be bothered by him. When we finally arrived at the house, I grabbed my son out of the car and went straight into the house. Devon and Rebecca were in the living room watching television. I walked straight past them and up the stairs to my son's room. I laid him in his crib and went back down the stairs. I walked around the house. The sink was full of dishes. The trash was not taken outside. I cleaned the house before I left. Now the house looked as if someone threw a couple parties and did not clean up the mess. I maneuvered around the mess and went upstairs to my son. I dressed him to go back outside. Marquis came into the room behind me.

"What's wrong with you?"

"What do you think?" I picked my son up and walked past Marquis who was standing in the doorway.

"Come on, we'll clean it. Where are you going?"

"I have some things I need to do. Plus I need to get out of this house before I kill one of you."

"I thought you were suppose to rest."

"I thought so too." I walked down the stairs as Marquis followed me.

"Leave him here. You don't need to take him out in that cold air."

"No, he's not staying here. He'll be just fine." I walked out the door and put my son in the car. Marquis stayed in the house and watched from the door. I ran a few errands and returned back to the house in the same condition it was in when I arrived the first time. I went straight upstairs and stayed there the rest of the night. Marquis and I began a downward slide in our relationship. We argued more often and barely talked to each other. He was gone more than he was around. I hated him.

A friend of Marquis and Devon's became my son's nanny. She was a great help to me. She asked for no money and stayed at the house. She also became my eyes when I was not home. She and I became good friends. She was only eighteen years of age, but very mature. I enjoyed being around her. She was a refreshing change. A couple of months later, when I could no longer stand living under the same roof as Devon, Rebecca and Marquis, I asked my nanny if I could move into her apartment. She did not hesitate to agree. A couple days later Marquis helped me move the large items into a storage unit and the rest went with me over to the nanny's apartment. I felt like freedom was almost in view.

Rebecca and Devon were upset with me for moving. They had no place to go. I was not concerned about it. Rebecca confronted me on one of my return trips to the house to make sure I had everything. I was already in a fowl mood and she just fueled the fire.

"Why didn't you tell us you were going to move?" She stepped up to me.

"I did, a month ago. You were probably too high to remember." I could see the anger build up in her face.

"Now where are me and my daughter supposed to live?"

"I don't know. That's not my concern."

"I thought you were a friend!" Her voice rose a little louder. For a minute I thought she might hit me.

"I thought you were too, but obviously not!" I turned to walk away. "You should have thought about your daughter when you were smoking that crap in the same room with your daughter! So don't give me that bull that you're worried about your daughter! Our friendship ended the moment you lied to me!" I turned and walked out of the house. She stayed where she was.

Over the next couple of days I saw Marquis off and on. I became unhappy with my whole situation. I wanted a change. At first I thought about actually moving back with my family, but then I realized they would not let me back with my second son. I finally made the decision to move. I just did not know where at first. On one of Marquis' visits I asked him about moving to Florida with his family. It did not take him long to say yes. The only problem he had was that he was still on probation for an old charge and had to stay in Ohio until it was over. I asked him if his family would mind if I went down ahead of him to get established. We called his mom and she agreed to let me stay with them until I could get settled.

I quickly made arrangements to move. I packed clothing into boxes and shipped them to Florida. I told my family I was moving. They were a little worried, but did not say much. I felt like I was given the opportunity to start new and fresh. On December 11, 1993, I left on a journey into unknown territory. I left behind every thread of who I was and where I came from. The child that left her parent's home when she was eighteen no longer existed. The person she had become was frightened and alone. I was somewhat anxious about driving with a three-month-old baby and two rottweilers. I decided it was the only way. The snow began falling at the beginning of my journey and did not end until I was well into Kentucky. After that I traveled until I was in Alabama and stayed in a motel over night. The following day I left early and finally made it into Florida that same evening.

I was nervous about meeting Marquis' family. I had met some of them before, but it was in Ohio. Now I was in Florida with them. I did not know how it would be. I called them a few times during my trip to give them my progress. I could tell Marquis' mom was excited about seeing her grandbaby. I began to believe I was doing the right thing. When I reached their house I was bombarded with more confusion. My son's grandmother was overprotective. I felt like I was incapable of making any correct decisions in her eyes. What little life I had left in me was snatched away in an instant. I felt I was overwhelmed and out of place. I became deeply depressed. I felt like a prisoner waiting the verdict of life in prison or death.

Marquis' mom made arrangements for him to come down to Florida for Christmas. I thought it would give us a chance to reconcile some of our differences. That was not the case. One of the girls he was seeing in Ohio called to talk to him constantly. I did not know how to handle it any longer. I almost felt betrayed. What hurt the most was that his mother knew that he was receiving the calls. The friction between Marques and I grew even more tense. I was in a state with no family. I had nowhere to go. I could not even go home. I decided to just lie back until I got my own place. Then I would be away from everyone. A few days after New Years Day, Marquis left to go back to Ohio. I was a bit relieved, but still wondered if he would return.

After he left I ended up in the hospital. I was having sharp pains in my side. I was at the hospital for six hours to hear I had an ulcer. If they had done an x-ray, they would have found that something very serious was wrong with me. The next day I had a nervous breakdown. The weight of everything on my shoulders was more than I could bear. I called my stepmother in California. She talked to me for a few minutes. One of her sisters lived only a few minutes away from where I was. She had her sister come and pick me up to spend some time with her family. The short visit helped a little. The next day I called and talked to my father who convinced me to come out to California to visit him for a month. I decided it would be a good idea. It would also give me the opportunity to rest some. He wired me a train ticket. I almost had to pull teeth to get someone to take me to the train station the day of my departure.

I never rode a train before and thought it would be fun. Little did I know how much trouble it would become. The train trip was shear torture. The pains that had sent me to the hospital became increasingly worse. I had no one to help me with my son. I could only sit for a short while before I needed to get up and walk. It is very difficult to maneuver on a moving train with a three-month-old child. I ate very little the entire train trip. The trip lasted three days. I was relieved to see my father in the parking lot waiting on my son and I. I still felt uneasy about seeing him, but anything was better than what I was going through. I was tired and wanted to go to sleep. My father had a dozen and one questions to ask. I politely answered them. After only a few minutes of driving we arrived at his home. My stepmother was anxiously waiting on our arrival. It was nice to see her. I had always liked her. She reminded me of my own mother. As much as my father complained about my mom, it amazes me that he married someone who resembles her and carries herself like my mom.

I was only in California a week before I had to have emergency surgery to have my gallbladder removed. The pain in my side had been a gallstone the size of a golf ball. I only had to stay in the hospital a few days. The doctor who preformed the surgery was worried that I had my gall bladder removed at the age of twenty-four. He told me it might do me some good to see another doctor when I arrived back home. He was worried about my depression and anxiety. Deep down I knew he was right. I knew what my problem had been and still was. I just did not want to start taking a ton of pills again. I was worried my successful remission off prescription drugs would end. I wanted to be clear-headed. I did not want to turn myself into a zombie like I had been in the past.

A day or so after my return from the hospital, California had a major earthquake. I believe the only thing that kept me calm was the darvacet the doctor had prescribed for pain. I had taken one before I fell asleep. My father's house did not suffer any damages to the structure, but the transformers outside his patio door blew up. It was quite a light show. The earthquake only lasted a few seconds, but it seemed longer. My father and stepmother had joined me in the living room. My step-mother held my son tightly in her arms. My father checked around the house to make sure everything was fine. He warned me there might be some tremors, but not to worry about them. He told me to go back to sleep. He would wake me if anything serious happened. When I felt safe, I finally dozed back to sleep.

A few hours later my father woke me up and asked if I still wanted to go to a local amusement park. I was a bit abased. I could not believe they would even be open. I told him I would. One of my distant relatives came and picked my son up to baby sit while my stepmother, my father and I went to the amusement park. I was amazed that the earthquake did not hinder the activities of the local residents. My father took the long way. He was worried about the integrity of the highways. The amusement park was full of people. I could not believe it. Every once in a while they would shut down an underground ride due to tremors. I never even felt them. Nonetheless, I enjoyed myself. I was able to forget everything that was going on in my life. I felt like a small child. We returned to my father's house late in the evening. My relative dropped my son off soon afterward.

I was enjoying myself in California, but I could not get Marquis off of my mind. I often called Ohio to see where he was. I called each one of the girls he was dating. It only offered me more trouble and grief. They began calling my father's house and harassing me. I became upset all over again. My stepmother helped as much as she could. She talked to me about it. She felt it would probably be in my best interest to leave Marquis. I knew she was right. I just did not want to face reality. Here I had moved to a strange state to get away from everything and it followed me. The only way the situation could be settled was if I faced it. I could not do that. Facing my problems would mean dealing with who I had become. I was not ready for that. As long as I was who I was, I had an excuse for my actions.

The time for me to return to Florida came quickly. Part of me wanted to return, but part of me wanted to stay where I was. My father took me to the train early in the morning. The train ride home was more enjoyable than the one to California. I felt like a pro at it now. I met and talked with a lot of people. Most of them were going to New Orleans for Mardi gras. The train was full of excitement. The train pulled up to the depot before the daybreak. Marquis' uncle was waiting for me. Marquis' sister had gone to the hospital for an emergency appendectomy. He took me straight to the house. I went to bed. I had some sleep deprivation from the trip. I was not given the opportunity to rest long. I was awoke and told to get up. I knew as soon as I got a job I would be able to move. All I had to do was hang on for a little while.

I was able to buy a car with my income tax check and I got a job soon after. I was scheduled to move into the apartment complex Marquis' mom managed. I was excited. I would finally have a place of my own. She put me in an apartment close to the office to keep an eye on me. I quivered every time I saw her coming. She would only stay for a little while to my relief. It was nice to be on my own. It had been a long time since I was on my own without anyone living with me. It was also the first time I was completely alone in taking care of a child. It was a new experience for me. I always had my grandparents or someone else to help me before. Now I was forced into being a mother. It was either do or die. I depended heavily on Marquis' mom telling me she would help me in any way she could. When I finally had to ask her to help me get to work because my car broke down, she turned me down. I felt abandoned. I soon realized how empty her words really were. I knew from that point on I could not rely on Marquis' family for any kind of help. I was truly on my own.

Marquis wound up in jail for a probation violation in Ohio. He had to finish his probation time in jail. I honestly felt more relaxed with him in jail. I knew his actions would be limited there. He called every night to talk to me. His female friends still harassed me. I hoped when he finally came down to Florida it would all end. How naïve I truly was. He finished his time the first week of April. A few days later he was on a bus to Florida. At first I did not think he was coming. I was frightened he would turn the tickets in for the money. I called the bus depot to see if he had gotten on the bus, but they could not tell me. The entire night one of the girls he was dating kept calling me telling me she was on her way down. She made it clear that Marquis had invited her to stay in Florida with him. I, of course, went off the deep end. I could not sleep the rest of the night. I was angry my sanctuary was going to be invaded by the same evil as before.

Upon Marquis' arrival I told him what had happened. He brushed me off. I just chose to ignore it. They were in Ohio still and he was with me. I was going to make an honest effort to give him a second chance. His uncle gave him a job where he was a manager. Everything went fine for the first few weeks. Marquis became restless again. He started going out. He started to stay away from the apartment. I just knew he was cheating. I started accusing him. Of course, he would deny it. We started arguing about it. The arguments became physical. We broke up and got back together quite a few time the next couple months. I could not understand it. I do not even know why I even let him back. I had no problems meeting other guys. I guess it was just something I was use to. I did not want to invest any more time into starting a new relationship.

Never fool yourself into thinking stress cannot kill you. I am surprised my stomach is still in one piece. I had become such a nervous person that I would go days without eating. I had anxiety attacks bad enough to send me to the hospital in an ambulance. My health was caving in on me. My doctor was very concerned for me. He made it clear that if I continued to live the same lifestyle I would be dead within a year. He prescribed five different medications to me. I reluctantly filled the prescriptions. It was the last thing I wanted to do, but everything else I tried failed. Taking the medications became my last and only resort.

I made sure I took the pills according to the instructions. I did not want to become dependent on pills any more. What happened, I did not expect. The pills took my independence away. I could not think clearly. All I wanted to do was sleep. Marquis would have conversations with me without my knowledge. Half of the time I did not know he was in the room talking to me. I became frightened something would happen to my son and I not know it. Marquis was surprisingly supportive. I think he liked the fact I was too cloudy minded to ask him any questions about his whereabouts. I soon realized that the pills did not offer any real improvement with the problems I was having. I slowly took myself off three of the prescriptions. I felt it was a waste of time and money for me to take something that was not working. Eventually I managed to pull myself off all of them.

Of course, with my full mental capacity back, Marquis and I continued our arguing marathons every Friday. I hated Fridays. I knew after he got home he would eat, take a shower, dress himself and go out for the night. Sometimes it would be the entire night. Some of the fights became physical. I would shove. He would push until one of us walked away. Usually it was Marquis. Marquis had a good heart, but had a real problem with being faithful. He always said the reason he was unfaithful was due to me constantly accusing him of cheating. Personally, I thought he could have come up with a better excuse than that. I had to try and come up with colorful excuses when people asked me why I was still with him. I never knew how to answer them. Sometimes, I just smiled and avoided the question.

Paul, one of his friends from Ohio, came down to stay with us to try and start a new life. I really did not want him around. I knew the problems we were having would only get worse. Paul's sister was one of the girls Marquis was dating the last couple of months I was in Ohio and until he moved to Florida. She still wanted to be with Marquis. She talked with him on the phone without my knowledge. Marquis told me of this some time later after we broke up. At this point in our relationship I did not care. Marquis got Paul a job where he worked. After a couple of days, Paul had to quit because of his allergies. I only worked three days a week. I was home a lot of the time with Paul a lone. It began to spark some jealousy in Marquis.

The lease to my apartment was going to expire soon. Marquis and I found a house by a friend of his that he played cards with all the time. The house had plenty of bedrooms for everyone. Marquis gave the deposit for the house. It came as a shock to me. Marquis was still lacking in that department. I still had to depend heavily on my income to pay for the bills. It only took a couple of days to move. After we moved everything to the house, I began cleaning the house and unpacking. We had no electricity or gas, but we made due. Marquis became increasingly jealous over Paul and I. He often came home for lunch to see what was going on. He always found us separate from each other. He started accusing us of being together while he was at work. This was one blow I refused to take. I was not even interested in Paul. The arguing escalated from there.

The whole relationship ended over a dog. I got a beautiful Eskimo dog from the pound. Marquis had already gotten one that he kept outside. I refused to let my dog outside. Marquis began to threaten me. I took the dog next door and called the sheriff. Upon returning to our house Marquis asked what I had done.

"I called the sheriff! I've had it with you!" I stood out in the yard in front of the porch. I knew not to get too close to him.

"Oh, you did!" Marquis disappeared inside of the house. The next thing I knew my stuff came flying outside. It was pouring the rain. It was also very cold out. My son was at his grandmother's. She had come and picked him up earlier in the day.

"You're going to jail this time!" He went inside of the house. Paul, a girl Paul was dating and Marquis came back outside together. They walked over to her car to leave.

"You're gonna pay for all my stuff! " That was the last thing I remember. A few seconds later, I was picking myself up off the ground. The three of them got into the car and left. The neighbors saw everything. When the sheriff arrived I pressed charges. I really had no choice. There were witnesses to a domestic violence offense. Marquis was taken to jail the moment he returned to the house.

I could not afford to live in the house by myself. I was virtually homeless. I did not know what to do. I wanted to go to Ohio, but the next-door neighbor convinced me to stay with her until I calmed down and thought everything through. The next day I decided to stay in Florida. I made arrangements to stay with Susan, the next-door neighbor, until I could find a place to live. I was able to apply for HUD due to being forced out of my home from domestic violence. I was given ninety days to find a place to live. I started counseling at a local domestic abuse center. After a couple of sessions I quit. Everything they were saying I had heard before. I wanted my entire past erased from memory. I did not want to reflect on it or even talk about it. I did not want to deal with the emotions I was going through. I just wanted them gone. Since they could not offer this opportunity to me, I felt it was just a waste of time.

Alcohol became my quick fix. It became my number one killer of bad memories. I was never the type of person to wait. Either it got done at the present moment or it did not get finished. Therapy was bothersome and too much work. I felt I was an intelligent enough person to work my own problems out. The only thing I could not see at the time was I had been trying to fix things on my own for the past seven years. I had seven years of garbage stacked in layers. Nothing I could ever have done would have cleaned the situation perfectly. I was blinded by stubborn pride. I needed help, but refused to believe it. I got angry with people who offered their unsolicited opinion. I did not believe they could help me. I mean how could they? They did not live my life. They did not know how I felt. I felt my life was more precious than wasting it talking to someone about things that could not be changed.

After a week of searching, I found the perfect place to move. It was out in the suburbs of town. It had a large fenced in yard like I was use to. It was a quiet area away from everyone and everything. I was absolutely thrilled with it. I was a little frightened to be on my own again, but I knew I would work it out. I had confidence things were going to turn around in my life. I only had a small amount of furniture and it only took a couple pick-up truckloads to move me. I settled into my new place quickly. I broke ties with almost everyone I knew. I made a ditch effort to change my lifestyle. I decided I did not need a man to survive. My baby boy and I could do well on our own. If I messed up, I messed up. I could only blame myself. I figured all the time to myself would be all the therapy I would need.

> *"Seest thou a man wise in his own conceit?*
> *There is more hope of a fool than of him."*

Proverbs 26:12

CHAPTER FIVE

"The way of the wicked is as darkness:
They know not at what they stumble."

Proverbs 4:19

****

A young man driving drunk was involved in a terrible car accident. His passenger was killed instantly. The young man was bleeding profusely from open wounds. The paramedics knew he would need to be given blood upon arrival at the hospital. Both the young man's parents and the passenger's parents were notified to come as quickly as they could to the hospital. The passenger's parents were the closest and arrived at the hospital first. The driver's parents lived over two hours away from the hospital. It still would be a while for them to arrive. The doctor took the passenger's parents into an empty room. The mother could tell something was wrong. Tears began to fill her eyes. She tried hard to control herself. She stuttered as she began to talk.

"How's my daughter?" The mother asked the doctor.

"I'm sorry, but I have bad news." The mother began sobbing hysterically. Her husband held her in his arms.

"Tell us doctor." The father interjected.

"Your daughter died in a car accident. She didn't suffer. She died upon impact."

"How did it happen?" The father asked wiping away tears from his cheeks. He held his wife tightly.

"The driver was drunk and the roads were wet. He lost control of the car and hit a tree. Your daughter was ejected from the car." The doctor's own eyes watered. He hated delivering news like this to parents.

"How do you know the driver was drunk? Couldn't he have just lost control of the car?" The father asked trying to find a valid reason for his daughter's death.

"The officers said they could smell the alcohol on his breath and the car was littered with beer cans. Of course, we will do a toxicology test to make sure."

"How is the driver? The father asked concerned.

"I'm afraid he's not doing too well. If we don't find him a donor in a short while, he will die."

"What kind of donor?" The mother asked releasing her grip on her husband.

"He has a rare blood type. We have none of it in storage. We paged the entire hospital. No one here has his blood type either. I'm afraid it does not look good."

"Where are his parents?" The mother asked.

"They live over two hours away. It will still be an hour or more before they arrive."

"What is his blood type?" The father asked.

"O negative," the doctor answered.

"No, you can't be thinking of helping him? He killed our daughter!" The mother became increasingly upset.

"I have O negative blood." The father said trying to comfort his wife.

"No, you can't! He killed our baby!" The mother cried aloud.

"If I don't help him, I will be just as guilty as he is. I'm the only one who can help him. Please understand." The father hugged his wife. She sobbed frantically. "Ok doctor, I'm ready."

"Follow me." The father followed the doctor out of the room. The mother fell into a chair crying.

Sometimes in life, we are involved in situations that make it hard to forgive the other parties involved. We want to blame them for everything and walk away never reconciling with them. We want them to hurt like we hurt. We want them to suffer life we suffered. The hardest thing in life to do is heal. It is painful, but we can make it easier if we forgive the people that have hurt us. Forgiveness is the key to all healing.

> *"Be ye merciful, as your Father is merciful.*
> *Judge not, and ye shall not be judged:*
> *Condemn not, and ye shall not be condemned:*
> *Forgive, and ye shall be forgiven…"*

Luke 6:35-38

Where would you be if God did not forgive you?

****

If you have ever been around small children playing with animals, you know how harsh they can unknowingly be toward the animal. The child believes he or she is just playing and is not harming the animal. Some animals graciously take the punishment out of love for their owners. While others will not. God recently showed me something through my daughter and a kitten I recently got. My daughter, of course, instantly took to the kitten. She terrorized the poor thing. I had to tell her constantly to leave the kitten alone. She would not. I have never seen a kitten take as much punishment as my daughter dealt out. I would have thought a cat would not take that much punishment. My first thought was that the moment my daughter let the kitten go, it would flee to safety. I could have never been so wrong. The kitten followed my daughter wherever she went. If for some reason the kitten could not get to her, she would meow until my daughter came and got her.

The kitten wanted attention so badly that it did not matter what kind of attention it received. All that mattered was that it received the attention, bad or good. At first I could not understand it until God started speaking to my spirit. I realized most of my life I looked for the same kind of attention from people. I did not care whether it was bad or good. All that mattered to me was that I received it. We all do the same thing. We all seek that unconditional child-like love even if means suffering some abuse to receive it. I judged my own self worth by the attention I received from other people. I suffered years of abuse, because I was searching for a love only God can give us, unconditional child-like love.

A month after I moved into my new place, I experienced my first hurricane. I did not know what to expect. I chose to stay at my house and not go to a shelter. We were without electricity for three days. Shortly after, when everyone became organized again, another hurricane swept through town. I left the house for this one, but came home during the middle of the storm. There was no damage to my home. We were only without electricity for a day. The small inconvenience did not bother me. It was a small wind- storm compared to the storms that have been brewing in my life. I felt I had my life in control. Little did I know that the difference between control and disaster was a very thin line.

It amazes me what I thought joy was then and what I know joy to be now. Peter said:

"...ye rejoice with joy unspeakable and full of glory..."

1 Peter 1:8

The joy God has given me is unwavering. It is joy unspeakable and full of glory. It is a joy that does not change because you are having a bad day or disappear through time. It is a joy that is never-ending. The joy God gives comes from within not from without. The joy the world gave me slowly cracked and broke into a million pieces. It is a like a brand-new car. At first it runs fine. Everyone compliments you about it, and the paint reflects everything. Through time, the paint begins to fade, the engine begins to have problems, and no one notices it any-more. Soon it becomes a hindrance to you. As time goes on, you have to work harder in order to keep it running properly. The joy the world gives is a joy that you have to work on constantly in order for you to keep it.

To earn extra spending money I started working at a local bar as a waitress. I made pretty good money. I started seeing a gentleman I had meant working there. He started calling after the second hurricane. I did not mind seeing him. He did not come over much at first. He gave me the little bit of freedom I needed. I knew how much of a playboy he was and decided to stay at a distance. I always got a bad feeling when I noticed him pulling into my driveway. Something kept telling me he was not being completely honest with me. I had a bad feeling that he was married or in a serious relationship with someone else. I asked him on several occasions if he was married or seeing someone else, but he always emphatically denied it. I gave him the benefit of doubt. I pushed the thoughts into the back of my mind. I was beginning to enjoy being around him and I did not want to ruin it. I thought all men could not be lying, cheating jerks.

Our time together increased gradually over time. He pampered me. I had never been treated like he treated me. He did everything a man should do. He was courteous and kind. He spent money without questioning me about it. He bought me clothing to go out in. He even paid for my son's babysitter on a few occasions. He threw me off balance. He was baiting me and I did not even know it. Just to be the center of someone's life was all I ever wanted. He offered that. No one else ever did. I slowly opened up to him. I noticed myself falling in love with him. I just did not let him know. I still could not get over the fact he was hiding something from me.

The crowning moment of the relationship was when he asked me to go to Daytona Beach with him. I wanted it special and spared no expense in doing so. We stopped in Georgia and stayed at his sister's house the first night. We all went out and enjoyed ourselves. All doubt of Scott being married disappeared for a brief period of time. Scott was more calculating than I had thought he was. The next morning we left for Daytona. We stayed over until Sunday morning and left. I drove back to Pensacola. I did not want the trip to end. The weekend excursion drew us even closer. I had fallen hard. I promised myself I would not, but it was too late. The thoughts of him being married surfaced every once in a while. I just pushed the thoughts to the back of my mind. Until I found proof, I just wanted to believe he was telling the truth.

Believing people and putting my trust in them has been a problem of mine every since I could remember. I always wanted to believe that everyone had some good in them. I could not believe that everyone was bad. I believed people should be honest and up front with each other. It is funny now that I think about it. I could not be honest with myself. I hid things from other people to avoid letting them see who I really was. I was a person who believed in the precious virtuous part of people, but yet, I did not believe I was precious enough to believe in myself. I did not believe in myself enough to be honest with others. It is stressful to hide secrets from people. It wears you down. You constantly have to watch what you are doing and who is watching you. You keep your enemies as friends and push away anyone who honestly wants to be a part of your life. You tell lies just to avoid the truth.

Scott was a heavy drinker. I never saw him without alcohol in his hands. He influenced me into drinking more than I already was. On top of the drinking I was not getting any rest. We went out and partied until the bars closed their doors. I began to have serious problems with my stomach. I had severe attacks. I discovered milk cured whatever was going on and kept on doing what I was doing. I should have stopped drinking all together. I rarely drank for fun. I normally drank to cover up the emotional strains I was going through. I was enjoying myself too much to think about my future health. I found a new me when I drank. This new person was not afraid to go out and have fun, to dance or take that extra chance. This new person did not worry about Scott sticking around or leaving the next day. I just lived for the day that was in front of me.

The holidays were quickly approaching. I wanted them to be special. I knew Christmas and Thanksgiving would be the true tests of his love. I would finally see what he was made out of. I went all out for Thanksgiving. I cooked the whole Thanksgiving meal. He came over and ate. He asked if I wanted to go out later. I agreed, of course. He told me he would return in a few hours. After I cleaned up from the meal I got ready to go out. After six hours he still did not show up. The feelings that he was married crept back into my conscious. Nine hours later he finally showed up. Like a dummy, I went. This is where I should have put my foot down. He knew I was upset, but he always had a way of saying things to calm me down.

His second test slowly approached. Christmas was coming and I was worried whether or not Scott was going to spend any time with me. He said he was going to Georgia to be with his family. I asked if I could go. After some thought, he finally agreed. Christmas eve he came over to spend the night with me so we could get an early start to Georgia. That night one of his clients called needing to go to the hospital. I went with him. I chose to sit in his truck while he went into the emergency room with his client. After a while I became restless and started looking through some of his mail. One of the envelopes was addressed to two people. His wife, I thought. I reasoned with myself. The name could be male or female. I reminded myself he had taken me to Georgia once and we were about to go again. After a few hours he returned to the truck. I said nothing to him about what I had found. We dropped his client off and returned to my house.

We got up early and opened our gifts. He bought my son some clothing and he got me a diamond ring. I was absolutely thrilled. After we ate breakfast, we left for Georgia. It took five hours to get there. I could not get over my Christmas gift. I thought I could not have been any happier. All the joy I had was stripped away from me after a brief conversation with his sister. The light I felt had brightened my life was turned off.

"I really like you. You're a nice person. I just don't agree with what my brother is doing." Of course, this grabbed my attention. I quickly fired a question at her before I lost the opportunity.

"What is your brother doing?"

"I believe he should make up his mind. Either he should get a divorce or leave you. Don't get me wrong. I hope he chooses you. His wife sticks to closely to him. She won't let him breath."

"I don't understand why he does it either." My insides boiled. I smiled at her and continued as if nothing was wrong. A few seconds later, Scott entered the house. He bent over and kissed me on the cheek. I wanted to wash my face where his lips touched me. I said nothing to him. I packed it down with all the other junk I had stored up throughout the years. He did not even suspect I knew. I said nothing the entire trip. The drive home was a long one. I had to make up my mind as to what I was going to do. We arrived at the house after what seemed like days. As we pulled into the driveway, I asked him what he was doing for New Years.

"I'm not sure yet, why?" I began to boil. I just smiled at him.

"Help me get my things out of the truck." He stayed for a few minutes and left. I got ready for work. I went to work with a heavy load on my shoulders. I could not concentrate on anything. After work I went home and just sat in the dark until I fell asleep.

My morality had slipped from me without my knowledge. When I look back now, I shutter. I cannot even imagine myself to be the same person. I should have cut all ties with him at once. I craved the attention he gave. I wanted something that was only going to turn out destructive to me. I was the strange woman Solomon talked so vividly about.

> *"For the lips of a strange woman drop as honeycomb,*
> *And her mouth is smoother than oil:*
> *But her end is bitter as wormwood, sharp as a two edged sword.*
> *Her feet go down to death: her steps go down to hell.*
> *Let thou shouldest ponder the path of life,*
> *Her ways are movable, that thou canst not know them."*

Proverbs 5:3-6

I can identify with her. I think about what her life must have been like. I wonder if the circumstances in her life were the same as mine. I wondered if all she ever wanted was for someone to love her no matter what it cost her.

I stepped from what was right onto the path of destruction. I changed my morals to fit the situation. I knew what I was doing was wrong. I knew that if I continued the relationship, I was no better than any other hooker on the street. Every moral fiber screamed, "No!" I reasoned with myself and came to the conclusion, why not? Everyone else was doing it. I thought this would be the perfect relationship. I have a saying; "The only thing perfect under the sun is God. The only thing perfect above the sun is God. Therefore the only thing perfect is God." Here I stood on the edge of a cliff. I could either walk away or jump off. To do what was right and to obey everything I was ever taught meant I needed to walk away. To ignore all that I have been taught, to go against my own beliefs, and to purposely hurt myself, meant I had to walk over the edge of the cliff.

I looked back at all the things I had been through. Then I looked at where I was headed. I decided stepping off the cliff was less painful than staying where I was. I disconnected myself with integrity and morality. I disregarded my actions as being irresponsible. It finally occurred to me that Scott still did not know I knew about his marriage. I became frightened he would leave me if I told him. I was actually worried a married man would leave me. What a joke! I should have been worried about what his wife would do to me. I made the decision to tell him I knew. I could not let him go on with his game any longer. I did not want him to play me for stupid any further. It was a few days before New Years when I decided to tell him. I sat him down and explained what I knew.

"I know that you are married."

"How many times do I have to tell you? I am not married." He smiled at me.

"Don't lie to me. Your sister told me your were married." The smile fell from his face. He looked down at his lap. Here it comes, I thought. I was never so wrong. What came out of his mouth still bothers me. For someone to be so indifferent amazes me even to this day.

"I am so glad you know. Now I don't have to hide it from you any more." I wanted to punch him.

"What about New Years?"

"What about New Years," he asked.

"Who are you going to spend it with?"

"Obviously, I need to spend it with my wife. She already told me she wants to go out." I was not going to go for that. If he was going to be with both of us, he was going to spend time with both of us.

"Why can't you spend it with me?" I was not expecting his answer.

"I guess we could. I guess we could work something out."

"OK," slipped from my lips. I do not even know who answered. It was like the word came out before I had time to even think of saying it. All three of us spent New Years together. She did not suspect anything was going on between Scott and I. She just assumed I was a co-worker and left it like that.

A few days into January, a job opportunity came open at Scott's place of employment. I applied and received the job. We now had a professional relationship, also. Discussions came up about him getting a divorce. It had gotten bad enough between his wife and him that he would bring his son over to my house for me to watch him. We had long discussions about removing the birth control I had in place. After a couple weeks of discussing it, the birth control was removed. Scott had promised if the summer went well between us, we would probably stay together. I thought he was a little bold to say it considering he was no were near getting divorce. I did not pay any attention to it. Scott and I continued to spend a lot of time together. The relationship became more intense. The drinking became more intense, too. Scott drank constantly. I just continued to follow his footsteps like a little puppy. He had a big influence on me. I could not see it at the time.

Scott began to complain I was not in shape. So, of course, to please him, I started working out. I went to the extreme like I normally do. I walked an hour a day. I lifted weights an hour a day and body sculpted for an hour a day. In two weeks, I saw visible results. I became obsessed with it. Scott's constant praises helped, too. I felt I now had an advantage over Scott. Other men noticed me more often, now. Scott noticed it, too. He became jealous. I loved it. My doctor on the other hand told me to slow down. He was worried my health would start declining. I actually felt better than I had ever felt before. Exercising gave me the energy I needed to hang out longer and drink more.

I thought I had conquered all the demons from my past. My self-esteem was back where it should have been. I had hope for the future. The hatred and anger was still buried deep within me. Scott left to go to a family reunion in southern Florida. I honestly felt like he had no right to go. I decided to go out with a female friend of mine. We stayed out all night over at one of her friend's. I knew Scott would call, but I did not care. It was time I turned the tables on him. When I got home Saturday morning, I had seven messages on my answering machine. He only called two other times the entire time he was gone. Upon his return, he came over to my house with a friend of his. I was furious. Scott and I got into an argument and he left. A few hours later Scott returned. I was angry enough to flip my glass tea table over. The glass shattered every-where. We exchanged a few words. On his way out he told me we were no longer together. I slammed the door behind him.

My first impulse was to tell his wife. Instead, I called a friend of mine. Before I could finish my conversation with her, he came back to the house to talk with me. I got off the phone with her and talked with him. He apologized and said he did not want to break up. I listened to his story of how much stress he was under and that he took it out on and me. Like a fool, I fell for it. I knew the relationship was doomed. I just did not want to come to the realization of it. He spent a few hours at the house before he left. I started to become cynical toward him. I was at a point now where it was going to be what I wanted or nothing at all. The stress of the whole relationship was taking its toll on me.

My son's great grandfather took him to New Orleans for the month of September. I became very ill the first week of September. I had to slow down with my exercising. I also lost all feeling in my hands. The doctor's could not explain why and put me on steroids. Scott was coaching his son's little league football team. Our time together was dwindling. When we did manage to see each other, it always ended in an argument. The fun was ending. I was confused. One moment I saw the advantages of a break-up. The next moment I did not want to be myself. I knew I could find someone else. I was given phone numbers all the time. I was just too afraid to let go of Scott. It was the comfort zone that had me trapped so many times before.

I was happy to see my son again at the end of the month. His great grandfather had finished potty training him. It was a relief to me. I had no patience to train him. A few days after my son's return, I became very ill. I had a feeling I was pregnant. I bought a home pregnancy test. It came up positive. I was nervous, but happy at the same time. I thought Scott would be happy too. It took me two hours to get in contact with him. The phone frightened me when it finally rang.

"Hello," I wanted it to be Scott on the other end of the phone.

"Why are you paging me?" I was relieved to hear his voice on the other end of the phone line.

"I have some news to tell you." I stuttered through my words.

"What is it?"

" I'm pregnant." There was a pause.

"You mean you have been paging me 911 for two hours just to tell me that?" Scott was angry.

"If you would have called me back the first time, I wouldn't have been paging you for two hours." I was angry. I could not believe his response.

"This isn't important. It could have waited until tomorrow," Scott angrily blurted out! I became furious and hung the phone up. I could not understand where I kept falling short. I even wondered why I kept putting up with my own behavior. I knew I could not tell my family. They were already upset with me. This would throw them over the edge. Depression became my best friend that night. I fell away from any sense of happiness.

Scott showed up the next morning asking what I was going to do. I quietly explained I was going to see my doctor to confirm my pregnancy and go on from there. He just looked at me. I could see his world crashing around him. Finally, I thought, someone else was having problems worse than mine. He left while I was taking a shower. I got ready and went to my doctor's office. Shortly afterward Scott showed up, too. Oddly enough my doctor's office was the very same one our job used for the employees to receive their TB tests. Scott showed up to received his TB test. He played it off acting surprised to see me there. I smiled and told him to leave me alone. The doctor confirmed my pregnancy. I left the office and said nothing about it to Scott. He paged me later and asked if he could come over and talk with me. I agreed. Later that evening after work he showed up at my house with a beer in his hand.

"Congratulations," he said sarcastically. "You finally got what you wanted." He leaned forward in the chair. "Have you thought about getting an abortion?" The words slipped off his tongue like silk. I just looked at him. I said nothing. "Well, I guess I'm gonna have to do all the talking since you have a problem." He started to recite rules to me. "First don't tell anyone I'm the father. Don't put my name on any of the paperwork." He paused for a second or two. "Since I believe you are telling me the truth, I'll give you $200.00 a month child support when the baby is born. Right now I'll give you $100.00 to help with the expenses." I listened as he rattled on. "You know this isn't fair? I believe it was those steroids you were on that got you pregnant. You know you still can have an abortion?" When he was done reciting his declaration, I recited mine.

"First of all, it was your idea to have the birth control taken out of my arm." I gently explained. "I have always kept protection here for you to use if you wanted to." I reminded him. "And on top of it all, if you did not want a baby outside of your marriage, you should not have committed adultery." He became upset with me and stormed out the door. I saw for the first time who he really was. He assumed I would do anything for him. He was only partially right. I was not going to kill my child for him. He was not worth it. His rules meant nothing to me. I protected myself. I told several friends and my son's family he was the father. They already knew I did not cheat on him. I had no time to cheat on him. He monopolized all my time.

The first half of the pregnancy went fine physically, but mentally I was having a difficult time. My depression became a real issue. I had three nervous breakdowns. I had several more anxiety attacks. He told me I was faking just to get attention from him. The attention I was receiving from him was the thing causing the attacks. I lost control over every emotion I had. I tried to go out and enjoy my life, but I could not. I feared I would see Scott in the bar with another girl on his arm or worse yet, his wife. I finally settled down and stayed at the house more often. By December, Scott and I broke up. The tension between us was tremendous. He kept a constant watch on me. He said he was protecting his investment. He was only protecting his skin.

I was doing fine until the last two months of my pregnancy. I began dilating and bleeding. The doctor knew I was under tremendous stress from my job. She just did not know the rest. I was in and out of the hospital until it came time to deliver. A week before I was due, my doctor decided to take me out of work and induce my labor. I was already four centimeters dilated. She was worried with it being my third child I might go into labor and deliver before I ever reached a hospital. My last two pregnancies caused her to be a little more alarmed than normal. I checked into the hospital early Saturday morning. My labor was to be induced at 3a.m. It was delayed until 5a.m. My next-door neighbor drove me to the hospital and stayed with me as long as she could. She had to go to work later that morning.

Once the procedure started I had to lay on my left side the majority of the time. It was extremely uncomfortable. The labor went slow and did not produce any results. One of the nurses and I watched horror movies together. About midday they increased the dosage of the drug to force my labor. My blood pressure worried the nurse. She went out several times to get a doctor to check me. She told me my blood pressure was not stable and needed to be watched constantly. It almost became a replay of my first son's birth. I was comfortable. I felt none of the contractions. By late evening I dilated to ten centimeters. I was ready to push. My doctor asked if she could call anyone. I explained to her that there was no one to call. Scott never showed up. He called once. He told me he was at a party with his family.

The next morning I woke up having severe chest pains. After an x-ray, I found out I had pneumonia. The nurses told me my daughter was ill, too. I grew worried for her and wanted her in the room with me. She stayed with me most of the day. Scott came and visited me later that afternoon. It was a short visit and I was happy when he left. I had grown tired of his pompous attitude. I only put up with him to receive my child support. His only worry was that his name did not appear on any of the paperwork. I doubt in the least bit that he even cared about his daughter or I. He reminded me of a criminal whose partner was put in prison and the only reason he went and visited him was to make sure he did not rat him out.

My regular doctor was called in due to my illness. He pleaded with me to call family members to help me. He threatened to call my mom to come down from Ohio to help me with the baby. I tried to explain my situation to him, but he could not believe my mother would never come down to help me. He prescribed medication for the pneumonia. I refused to take anything for depression. My only problem was I needed to take control of my life. I needed to stop letting other people control my life. I went home a few days later. I was nervous about my new life. I now had to be responsible for two children. I wondered if I could do it. I knew I had to keep a level head. I knew I had to take things in stride. I had to straighten up.

I returned to work the first week of July. Two weeks later I was fired. My supervisor told me I was not needed any longer. I was upset. I kept calm and levelheaded. I took the precautions I needed to. I looked at it as an opportunity to start all over again. I would be able to pull myself further from Scott. I enrolled in a program for displaced workers. I started technical school in August. I distanced myself further and further from people. I felt like things were going to start turning around for me. By April of the next year, I was running my own landscaping business. I had plenty of customers. I was enjoying myself. I started dating again. I did not want a serious relationship. I was not ready for that. I was now twenty-eight years of age. It had been ten years since I became an adult. It felt like fifty. Nevertheless, no matter what storms I had weathered, I was still hopeful for the future.

CHAPTER SIX

"Hath not the potter power over the clay, of the same lump
To make one vessel unto honor, and another unto dishonor?
What if God, willing to show his wrath, and to make his power known,
Endured with much longsuffering the vessels of wrath fitted to destruction:
And that he might make known the riches of his glory on the vessels of mercy,
Which he had afore prepared unto glory.
Even us, whom he hath called, not of the Jews only, but also of the gentiles.
And he said also in Hosea, I will call them my people,
Which were not my people; and her beloved, which was not beloved.
And it shall come to pass, that in the place where it was said unto them,
Ye are not my people; there they shall be called the children of the living God."

Romans 9:21-26

****

A man was opening a brand new store. It was something he planned all his life. A month before the store opened, he hired four young boys to pass out fliers for advertising. Everyday they would come faithfully to pick up the fliers to pass out. At the end of the day they returned to the store to receive their pay. The owner of the store continued this ritual until the store's opening day. On the day of the grand opening, the owner gave the young boys fliers with coupons as an extra incentive. The boys left the store to pass out the fliers. After the store was opened for a few hours, the store still did not have any customers. He became worried. Just when he decided to close the store for the day, a customer came into the store. In the customer's hand were a handful of fliers.

"Good morning. How are you?" The store's owner had a giant smile on his face. He was happy to see a customer.

"I'm fine." The customer placed the fliers on the counter.

"What's this?" The owner asked. He pulled the fliers closer to himself.

"These are fliers from your store. For the past month I have watched four young boys dump these in a trashcan in from of my store. At first I did not think anything about it, but today I decided to see what they were. I brought them to you to make you aware of it." The customer turned around and walked out of the store. The storeowner became furious. He stayed until the four young men returned at the end of the day to receive their pay.

"How'd you guys do today?" The owner asked them as they approached.

"Fair," one of the boys answered. The owner placed the fliers on the counter. Their eyes fell on the fliers.

"Do you know what these are?" The owner asked the boys.

"Where did you get those?" Another boy asked the owner.

"I gave you a simple job to do. I paid you well for it. Obviously you thought it wasn't important enough for you to do. I wanted to offer you gentlemen jobs in the store when the store opened. I guess that's out of the question now. You boys can leave my store."

"We're sorry. How can we make it up to you?"

"It's too late, now. I'm already open. I had no customers in my store today because of your inconsideration. Please leave."

Jesus left us with a few commandments.

> *"Thou shalt love the Lord thy God with all thy heart,*
> *And with all thy soul,*
> *And with all thy mind."*

Mathew 22:37

The second commandment was:

> *"Thou shalt love thy neighbor as thyself."*

Mathew 22:39

When we accept Jesus Christ as our salvation, we are obligated to announce to everyone we meet about his salvation. Everyday God gives us blessings and mercies beyond our worth. It is our responsibility to pass them out to everyone else.

> *"Go ye therefore, and teach all nations,*
> *Baptizing them in the name of the Father,*
> *And of the Son and of the Holy Ghost:*
> *Teaching them to observe all things whatsoever I have commanded*
> *you:*
> *And lo, I am with you always,*
> *Even unto the end of the world. Amen."*

Mathew 28:19,20

When you are out in public around other people, do you throw away what God has given you or do you pass it out to everyone you come in contact with?

****

During my relationship with Scott, I had ignored my son and his needs. I was never shown how to be a mother. I found it very difficult to relate to him. I found myself treating my son like my mother did my sister and I. I felt I was being a mother because I clothed, fed and took care of him. My son needed my emotions. He needed by hugs and my love. These were things that I had given away to people who never gave them back. I was emotionally drained. I was unstable in my ways and I knew the children could sense this. This pushed me even further from my son. I could see clearly that my son was in desperate need of help. His behavior became worse after my daughter was born. I heard him voice on numerous occasions that he wanted to kill me. I was afraid for my son, my daughter and I. I knew all too well where his behavior could take him. I desperately sought for help. I found none. My options were to wait until he turned five or wait until he physically hurt someone on three separate occasions. I began to come to the realization that most of his behavior was a result of the life I lead.

I did not know how to be a mother. I was frustrated and alone. My anger controlled my life. I did not want to be bothered with my children. I wanted to live my life. I thought it was unfair that my children's fathers had no cares for them. They did not have to worry about feeding, clothing, or taking them to the hospital. I saw my mother in me. I began to understand how she must have felt at first after her divorce from my father. The only difference was that I had no one to take my children off of my hands what I needed a break. I could not just leave and go out when I wanted. I was selfish, and I believe at times I only put up with my children because I had to. My children came in fourth after me, myself, and I. I never considered the effects a decision would have on them. I just made the decision.

My business was doing fine and I thought I was heading in the right direction. That was until June of 1998. My grandmother passed away unexpected. She broke her hip a short time before. A blood clot traveled from somewhere in her body and moved to a dangerous spot. She died minutes later. My mother called me with the news. I was in shock, of course. Tears welled up in my eyes. Not My grandmother, I thought. I hung up with my mother and went back to bed. It was 7a.m. I had just gotten home a couple hours earlier. After the initial shock past, I could not find any more tears. The memory of her methodically taking my older son from me and telling me I was not welcome there anymore invaded my thoughts. I even wondered if she was going to heaven.

After debating whether or not I should go, I called my mother to see if she could help me get to Ohio. My business was doing well, but it was the middle of the month. My clients normally paid me at the beginning of each month. I had no extra money put aside. My mom told me she could not help. I became desperate. It was now important for me to go. I called my father who decided to help me reluctantly. I called my mother and told her I was able to come to Ohio. I asked her if I could stay with her. She told me no. My heart sank. My own mother was turning me away. I yelled and cursed at her in anger. She told me none of my relatives had room for me. I told her I would sleep in the car with my kids if I had to. I hung the phone up and started calling my dad's side of the family. Everyone, but one of my uncle's said no.

I gathered what I could and packed the car. I was worried about traveling to Ohio with two small children. Nevertheless, I knew I had to make the trip. I kept telling myself God would help me get there safely. I knew how long the trip was. I was already upset and I knew my mind would not be on driving. My window on the driver's side was broke and would not go up. I did not expect the weather to turn as bad as it did as I approached Ohio. It rained the majority of the way to Ohio. It was 55 degrees and raining once I reached Ohio. It felt like winter. I arrived at my uncle's in the evening. I hurriedly unpacked the car and got ready to go to my grandfather's house. I really did not want to go. I had not seen my grandfather in four years.

I was absolutely terrified to go to my grandfather's house. I did not know what to expect. I did not think he would want to see me. My uncle lived quite a distance from my grandfather's house. It was a long drive. I had time to prepare myself mentally. When I arrived at my grandfather's house my sister, her husband, my aunt, my grandfather, and my oldest son were there. I was even more nervous about seeing my son. I did not know how he would take me being around him. My mom and her husband had just left before I arrived. Everyone greeted me warmly. My son was a little shy. I already expected that. My feelings were not hurt. It did not take long for my two sons to get acquainted. They went outside to play. It was awkward talking to my grandfather. I had gone through so much since he saw me last. I felt like a giant canyon was dug between us. I was no longer the innocent little girl he once knew. I felt dirty in his presence. Knowing my family did not want me there made it worse. My sister asked a million and one questions. This was not out of the ordinary for her. My grandfather retired early. My aunt and I went outside and talked for a few minutes.

I asked if I could invite a friend I grew up with. My aunt did not mind. I called her and she came right down. She only lived a few blocks away from my grandfather's house. Only a few minutes into our conversation, I could see how bitter she had become. She had lost four children from miscarriage or death. She blamed God. She said she hated him. Her last statement throttled my thoughts. I tried to explain to her that it was not God's fault. I could feel my soul cry out for her. I did not know what to say or how to help her. With everything I had gone through, I was incapable of helping her. I already felt as if she was doomed. Not once did I ever blame God for my life. It was almost as if I knew I had to live through the things I had gone through. We talked for a little while longer, and then she left. I felt an uneasy feeling for my friend. I could not understand why she had so much hate for God and I had none. My aunt went inside to go to bed and I went back to my uncle's to get some sleep.

When I woke up the next morning, my stomach was turning with knots. I had not seen my family since I left for Florida. I did not know how they were going to react to my children or I. I felt like a lamb going to the slaughter. I tried to prepare myself mentally for what I thought would happen. Surely, I thought, my family would put aside any differences there was. I got the children and I ready and left my uncle's house. I went to have my care looked at and then went to find a dress to wear to the wake. I had forgotten to pack two dresses. There was a little chill in the air. My children only had shorts to wear. The city I had grown up in had changed a great deal. I could not believe all the stores that have been built. I almost got lost. After searching for a little while I finally found a dress. I went to my grandfather's house to get ready.

The house was full of people when I got there. I tried to stay out of sight as much as possible. I did not want to be seen by anyone. I did not think I could handle their snide remarks or dirty looks. I was asked to move my car for someone to leave the driveway. I went outside to move it. I left my children in the living room. It was raining outside and I did not want to take them outside. I did not see any harm in leaving them inside the house. I was wrong, of course. The last person I would expect to say something to me did. My sister met me in the kitchen when I entered back into the house.

"What right do you have to leave your children in this house? Everybody is already upset! Then you leave your kids crying in the living room! Nobody wants to hear that! You don't even belong here! I was here for grandma! You weren't!" Her words ripped through every part of my body.

"Did you expect me to take my kids outside in the rain just to move my car? Now get out of my face before I say something I will regret!" I was upset. A few of my relatives were standing in the kitchen. My sister stormed out of the kitchen crying. I had tears in my eyes, but refused to let them see me cry. I told my kids to follow me and I went to the back of the house out of sight. After I got dressed, I went to the rec-room to gather my belongings and to get my kids ready. Outside I saw my mom and her husband pull up. My grandfather came to the rec-room to greet them. I at least expected my mom to sat hello, but she never even acknowledged me.

"Your daughter is here." My grandfather said. She smiled at my grandfather and walked into the living room. I could not hold back the tears any longer.

"Grandpa, if you want me to leave, I will." I was so upset I could barely get the words out.

"You're always welcome, here. You know that." The problem was that I did not feel welcome in the home I had spent eighteen years of my life in. I felt like a stranger. I finished getting the kids ready and put my stuff in the car. I stayed outside of the house until it was time to leave for the funeral home.

I know how Mary felt when she walked into the room with all those people watching her. They whispered to each other. They scorned her with facial expressions. I knew how she felt when she knelt at Jesus' feet to wash them. I know the tears that washed his feet. I have cried the same tears. The tears of lost dignity, the tears of broken dreams, the tears of lost innocence, and the tears of shame are the same tears that filled my eyes. She lowered herself to raise herself. She humbled herself in front of people who took every shred of humanity from her and told the God she wanted to worship she was worthless. I know how she felt. I knew what I was in for when I left Florida, but sometimes you just hope people are not that cruel, but like Mary I walked into a den of lions and humbled myself so that one day I could be raised from my weaknesses.

After everyone arrived at the funeral home for the wake, I felt like I was in a room of strangers. I sat in the back of the room by myself. I let my son play with his older brother and a few cousins. I was afraid to let him play without me there to protect him. Occasionally, someone would come up to me and say hello. I could see their looks and hear their whispers. When I had almost given up hope all my entire family, two angels came to my rescue. My grandfather's sister and her daughter came and sat beside me. My cousin knew what I was going through she had married a black man and had two children by him. She lost a good job at a university from it. She knew what it was like for me. She and my aunt helped me with the children a little bit. I was relieved. They were a great help to me. I needed it. Their act of kindness actually helped me get through the rest of the wake.

I left the wake before everyone else. I dropped by a fast food restaurant and got the kids something to eat and went back to my uncle's house. The drive to his house gave me some time to cool off. My uncle was at the house when I arrived. He knew it was going to be hard for me. He knew how my family could be. He greeted me as I came into the door.

"How did everything go?" He asked as I came in.

"Well, I now know where I rank in my family."

"Where's that?"

"No where." I smiled at him and started to walk up the stairs.

"Was it that bad?"

"Yep," I hollered back down the stairs as I continued up them. I turned to look at him. I could see he had something in his hand.

"Here, I thought you might want this." He lifted his hand toward me to hand me something. I came partially down the stairs to get it. It was my grandmother's obituary.

"Thank you." I took the clipping out of his hand and went upstairs. I waited until I got into the room before I read it. It was the final blow written in words for the entire world to see. My two youngest children were not mentioned in the obituary. It had only mentioned she had one great grandchild. I started to cry. I laid in bed most of the night thinking. I knew how to turn off my emotions when it came to everyone else, but I could not do it with my family.

The next morning, when I awoke, the rain was coming down hard. It was almost freezing. I had no warm clothes for my kids. I made sure I left some blankets out for them. I knew they would need them. I got ready. My uncle was already up. He was giving my son some orange juice. I packed the bags and put them into the car. I had made the decision to go home after the funeral.

"I'm gonna leave right after the funeral. I won't be coming back here."

"Are you sure you won't need to stay another day?" My uncle looked concerned for me.

"What for? My family doesn't want me here." I paused for a second as tears came to my eyes. "I want to thank you for your help. I really appreciate it."

"No problem. Be careful on your way home."

"I will." I prepared the kids to go outside and put them in the car. I hugged my uncle and left.

I had some time to think as I approached the funeral home. I went straight there. I went in and sat with my family in the front. My son began to wonder around. I, of course, became upset. I knew my family would not allow it. It did not take long before it was suggested I move. I moved away from them. I retreated to the back of the room, again. I wondered if anyone cared that it was my grandmother who died, too. People walked by me and said nothing. I have never felt so alone as I did that day. I felt like an outcast. I felt more hate growing inside of me. I went outside to smoke a cigarette. I stayed outside until the funeral procedures were over with and went back in.

"Are you going to the burial site?" It was one of my aunt's.

"I want to." I said.

"Well, make sure you and the kids stop by and get something to eat." She smiled and hugged me.

"OK." I was pleasantly surprised with her kindness. She was one of the last ones I expected to be kind to me. I expected one of my family members to invite me to ride in the limo with them, but they did not. I was left to drive to the gravesite behind the limo. I was given no family privileges the entire funeral. Only two or so people came up to console me out of fifty or more guests. I felt like I was a shadow. After the funeral, the funeral attendants handed out flowers from my grandmother's casket. I stood there waiting for mine. They did not hand me one.

"Give the other granddaughter one." I heard someone say.

"Who is she?" The attendant asked.

"Here I am." I reached my hand out for the flower. It was a carnation. They were my grandmother's favorite flowers. I followed some family members to my aunt's house. It was only a couple of miles from the burial site. When I got there, I sat in the living room with my children. My aunt and cousin sat with me.

"Go and get something to eat for you and the kids. We'll watch them until you return." My cousin took my daughter and motioned me to go. I smiled and got up to get their food and mine. I sat back down and tried to eat. My sister sat next to me.

"I'm sorry about those things I said. I was upset." I glanced up at her. I did not want to answer her, but I felt like I had to.

"Don't worry about it." I wanted to tell everyone in the room to step off a cliff. My grandfather, the man I adored, was the only thing that kept me from saying anything to anyone. I took the ridicule, the cruel words, gestures and looks for him. I loved him too much to lash out at anyone. I knew their actions were caused from ignorance and the unwillingness to except people for who they are.

My mom, who already dealt one low blow, took it even further. My younger son, who is a very affectionate person, took my mom's hand and asked her what her name was. My mom got up and pulled her hand from my son's.

"What's your name?" He asked, again.

"Connie," she answered and walked away. I was no longer hurt by my mother's actions. I was angry. I felt she had no right to treat my son like that. She could say anything she wanted to me, but not to my son. He never did anything to her. She was his grandmother whether she liked it or not.

"Are you going to let her get away with that?" My sister asked. I was surprised my sister said anything about it at all. "Well, are you?" I said nothing in return.

After the kids and I finished eating, I let my son play with his older brother. I tried to talk to some of my relatives, but I felt out of place talking with them. I finally decided to go ahead and leave. I asked my aunt for a room I could change my clothes in. She showed me to a guest's room. I sat on the couch and bawled my eyes out. After I calmed down, I hurriedly changed my clothes and changed my daughter's diaper. I could not wait to get away from my family. After I put my things in the car, I came back into the house to say goodbye to my grandfather. He was sitting in the living room with my sister and mom.

"I need to leave." My grandfather looked up at me and stood up.

"You don't have to leave now if you don't want to." Tears filled his eyes. I could not stand to see him cry.

"No, I need to get home. I have some clients that are waiting on me."

"Do you need any money?" My grandfather never stopped worrying about me.

"No, I'm alright." We hugged. I did not want to let go of him. I feared it would be the last time I would ever see him alive. My sister, mom, and a few other family members hugged me as I walked out of the door. I called for my son, who took his good old time coming.

"Wait," a voice called from behind me! I turned to see my aunt running toward me. "Here's some food. Take this." She handed me some money. I tried to give it back to her but she would not take it. "It's not much, but it will help some. You are always welcome here. Come back to see us sometime, alright?" She hugged me as my son approached the car. I got him belted in as the rain began to poor, again. I pulled out of the driveway and headed for a gas station. I was relieved, but at the same time I did not want to leave. I knew Ohio was no longer my home. It was just the place where I grew up. It's just a place my family lives now. My life was in Florida.

Sometimes, when I look back over my life, I wish I were a child, again. Not because I would not have any responsibilities, but for the sake of not knowing the cruelty of life. Or maybe, just to believe that love was unconditional and not painful. I do not blame my family for anything that has happened. Nor do I condemn them. They were only doing what was right in their eyes. God told Samuel:

> *"...For the Lord seeth not as man seeth; for man*
> *Looketh on the outward appearance,*
> *But the Lord looketh on the heart."*

1 Samuel 16:7

My family was looking at my outward appearance. They were looking at my actions. They were seeing what the outward man was doing. They could not see what the inside man was doing. The inside man just wanted the love it deserved. The inside man wanted someone to dig out all the junk that had accumulated and remove it. The inside man wanted to be the child again that everyone loved unconditionally. The inside man wanted to be the child that never hurt it's family by it's actions.

Where I lacked with my family, I lacked with God. I could not believe God could love me or forgive me unconditionally. I did not believe I was worthy of God's love or forgiveness. Even after I was saved, I thought if I held back the attributes God would be ashamed of, he would love me. I knew God knows everything. I guess it was just a comfort zone for me. It took a while for me to realize that God is willing to call me his child knowing all the dirty little secrets I have. He saw my heart. God knew who I was and still He loved me.

I gave up worrying about my family mid way through my trip home. It grew warmer the closer I got to Florida. It was 103 degrees when I finally arrived at my house. It was a drastic change in temperature. The cold reception I received in Ohio was met with the warmth of a state where I had no family. I brought the kids in from the car. They were tired from the trip. I took them in and put them to bed for a nap. I left my belongings in the car. There were several messages from customers and friends. I decided to wait until Monday to call anyone. I needed the rest and did not want to be bombarded with questions. I lied down on the bed and fell asleep. I was exhausted mentally and physically. A week or so later, my doctor informed me I could not longer stay outside without being in danger of receiving skin cancer. I had sun poisoning already five times before. I had to give up my business. My customers were a little upset. My heart was not in it any longer since my grand-mother's death. It was a choice that was going to come sooner or later, anyhow.

CHAPTER SEVEN

*"Jesus answered and said unto her, If thou knewest the gift of God,
And who it is that saith to thee, Give me to drink;
Thou wouldest have asked of him, and he would have given thee
living water.
The women saith unto him, Sir, thou hast nothing to draw, and
the well is deep:
From whence then hast thou living water?
Art thou greater than our Father Jacob, which gave us the well,
And drank thereof himself, and his cattle?
Jesus answered and said unto her,
Whosoever drinketh of this water shall thirst again:
But whosoever drinketh of the water that I shall give him shall
never thirst;
But the water that I shall give him shall be in him a well
Of water springing up into everlasting life."*

John 4:10-14

****

A woman, who had a perfectly normal pregnancy, went to the hospital to have her baby. Everything was going fine until it was time to deliver. The doctor noticed the baby was turned the wrong way. After examining the mother, the doctor noticed the mother was bleeding internally. The doctor knew the situation was critical. The doctor had to make the decision to remove the baby immediately or the mother would die. The doctor explained the situation to her.

"Sweetie, we need to perform a emergency c-section. Your baby is physically fine. He is just turned the wrong way. You, however, are bleeding internally from an unknown source. I cannot find it. If we do not perform the surgery soon, you and the baby will die." The woman became nervous. Tears filled her eyes. She hesitated for a moment. Then she answered the doctor.

"Doctor, all my life I have screwed things up. Then I receive the opportunity to bring a life into this world. I can't screw this up. I love my baby more than this world. If it comes down to it, save his life not mine. If he dies, I might as well, too." The young woman said trying to hold back her tears. The doctor could not believe what she had just heard.

"Are you sure about this?" The doctor asked skeptically.

"Nothing will change my mind." The young girl closed her eyes.

"I'm not going to let you go that easily." The doctor said as she began calling all the necessary staff. The young woman was wheeled into the operating room. The doctor started the operating procedures. Everything was going wonderfully. The doctor became confident the young girl would survive the surgery. She was able to find the source of her bleeding and stitched her up. After the young girl was stabilized she was handed her baby by one of the nurses. The young girl smiled at the staff and whispered in her baby's ear.

"You're my greatest gift. I will love you always. Grow and be strong." The young girl closed her eyes. The alarms went off. The nurse hurriedly took the baby from the girl. The hospital staff tried to resuscitate her. Every attempt failed.

"She knew she was going to die." The nurse holding the baby said.

"She loved him enough to die for him." The doctor answered.

God loved us enough that he gave up his only son, so we could have eternal life.

> *"For God so loved the World that he gave his only begotten Son,*
> *That whosoever believeth in him should not perish*
> *But have everlasting life."*
>
> John 3:16

God, through his Son, let us know that he would do anything for us. He has a love so great for us that it surpasses all understanding.

> *"This is my commandment, that ye love one another, as I loved*
> *you.*
> *Greater love hath no man than this,*
> *That a man lay down his life for his friends."*
>
> John 15:12,13

Would you give up a child so a stranger, a friend, or a family member could live? God made the ultimate sacrifice, could you?

****

About six months before I had gotten save, I worked at a floral nursery. I was cleaning and getting the greenhouse ready for spring. On one particular day, I was working on citrus trees when I noticed a small scrawny tree barely sitting in the pot. For some strange reason, I felt compassion for the tree. By all reasons the tree should have been thrown away. I took the tree inside and asked the owner's wife if the tree was worth keeping. She examined the tree.

"It has thorns and no real root system. It won't produce any good fruit. It has reverted back to its wild state. Throw it away." She hand the tree back to me.

"Can I have it?" I asked feeling sorry for it.

"Yes, if you want it? Don't let my husband see you take it outside." I put the tree in a paper bag and placed it in my car. When I got home that evening, I planted the tree in a good pot, with good soil. I fertilized it, trimmed it and watered it. I protected it and watched its progress daily. The following summer the tree bloomed, but never produced any fruit. I decided to wait until the next summer to see if it would produce any fruit.

The next summer the tree bloomed, again. After the blooms fell off, I waited. When I was about to give up, I noticed a small marble sized fruit on one of its stems. I was elated. It only produced one fruit, but that did not waver my excitement. The fruit grew over time and became ripe. One morning as I was getting ready for church, God began to speak to my heart. He spoke to me about the lemon tree I have had so much patience with.

"Remember the lemon tree and how you saved it from death. You kept it from being thrown out? That was you. The world had thrown you away. You were worthless to it. It could not use you anymore. I picked you up out of the trash. I planted you. I fertilized you. I trimmed you. I watered you. I waited, also, for you to blossom and produce fruit. It might be one fruit now, but in time it will become more than your branches can stand. Your roots need to grow strong in order to support your growth.

The few months before I became saved I continued to pull myself from the people I normally hung around. I felt out of place and unwanted. It was hard for me to cope at this point. Sometimes, I wondered if I was resisting the change I felt happening in my life. It is difficult to explain. It is as if one moment I was molded into one image and then half way through I was being torn down and changed into another image.

> *"And the vessel that he made of clay was marred in the hand of the potter:*
> *So he made it again another vessel, as seemed good to the potter to make it."*

Jeremiah 18:4

I was confused and desperately seeking answers. I knew things were changing. It was out of my hands. Something was happening I had no control over. I did not feel threatened by the change. I just resisted it. It was like growing from a child to adulthood. You knew it was happening, but sometimes you just did not like how it felt.

I felt my old life slipping away from me. I felt the spark of a new one smoldering deep within. The person I was and the life I was leading was no longer viable. I was walking the path of fools. I almost let the world crumble me under her fist. My whole life I knew there was something better. All I had to do was wait for it, not run from it. Most of my adult life I had spent on my knees crawling, barely hanging on to what life I had in me. It was time for me to stand up. I was tired of being a victim. I was tired of punishing myself. I was tired of resisting who I really was. It was time for me to dust myself off, take inventory, and go on. It was time for me to face the reality that was giving to me and do my best with it.

I stayed withdrawn from everyone. I figured if I did not put myself in the position to get hurt, I would not. I even withdrew myself form my children. I went through the basic mechanics with them. I had no emotions to show them. My emotions were still unstable. I was probably manic-depressive, but I refused to get checked. I did not want to be on any more medications. I knew that path too well. I was clean and wanted to stay that way. I was looking for answers, but no one wanted to hear the questions. I did not know where I was going in life. I did not understand the changes occurring around me. I was tired of exerting myself for anyone. I focused on the present. There was no looking back or forward.

Without notice, God placed someone in my life that would direct me to the right path. His name was Deondre' He had grown up in the church and was still going. This impressed me. We talked on the phone at first. It soon developed into a relationship. We saw each other on a daily basis. Deondre' rekindled the flame I once had. I could feel my heart grow warmer for the man I had so much compassion for years ago. The world tried to put the flame out that God had placed inside of me over twenty years earlier. It now was building into a raging fire again. I started to ask questions. I started to read and study the bible. Deondre' answered as many questions as he could, but our conversations normally ended in arguments.

I was firm in my decision to learn about God, but Deondre' was not equipped to help me. The first problem was that we grew up in different churches. Second, he was firm in his beliefs, but he did not practice them. He picked up his religion to exert a fact or justify an action. I was used to Christians doing what the world did. His behavior did not seem out of order to me. He went out to the clubs, he listened to music that was questionable, and he allowed himself to be persuaded by someone who was not saved. Because of this, he could not witness to me effectively. I saw no separation between the world I knew so well and the church that was able to save my soul.

I yearned to go to church. It became an obsession. I asked Deondre' constantly if I could go with him. He turned me away consistently. One day after I dropped Deondre' off at his church, I got this over-whelming desire to go to church. I went straight home, dressed the kids, and got myself ready. I decided to go to my friend's church. I was an hour late, but I still went in. I knew I made a step in the right direction. It felt good to be there. After the service was over, I went to pick up Deondre' from his church. All I could do was smile when he got into the car.

"What's wrong with you?" He asked.

"Guess where I have been." I could not stop from smiling.

"I don't know, tell me." He gave me a strange look.

"Come on, guess."

"I don't know." When I saw he was not going to guess, I blurted it out.

"Church."

"Church. You went to church? Worship, God, Preaching church?" A look of amusement came over his face.

"Yes." I pulled out of his sister's driveway to go home.

"You're pulling my leg?"

"No, I'm not. I went to a friend's church."

When we got back to the house, he asked me again. I knew I had taken a step in the right direction. I dived in with utter enthusiasm. The empty space in my heart did not seem as empty. I read my bible for hours at a time. I searched for the answers to the questions I had. I soon came to the realization that I need to be baptized. No one at the church I was attending tried to witness to me. I had to ask how I would go about becoming baptized. That same Sunday, the kids and I stepped to the front of the church to become members and be baptized. I should have known something was wrong the moment they scheduled a day for me to get baptized. My lack of knowledge kept me from questioning what was going on.

I asked Deondre' to go with me thinking he would be thrilled to see me baptized. He threw a fit. I thought he would be more gracious about it. The whole baptism was marred by his attitude. All I wanted was his support and I did not even get that. After the baptism the pastor asked him to stand. He grew even angrier with me. He refused to talk with me. After the services the pastor came to talk to me about some of the ministries the church had to offer. He told me he would like me to join the ladies group. My work schedule kept me from joining. I really did not feel comfortable joining any of the ministries. As a whole the church never really made me feel comfortable at all. At times I was asked to move out of a long time member's seat. I refused to quit over people's attitudes. I continued to go regardless of how I was treated. It was the pastor's behavior that would eventually stop me from going to the church.

A week or two after I got baptized, I felt the need to talk to the pastor about my life. He seemed a bit confused as to the reason I wanted to meet with him. It was almost as if he had never had a conference with any of his parishioners. He set an appointment anyhow. I was anxious to see him. I thought I would finally be able to lye my past to rest. I was not prepared for what was going to happen. I went over everything that had gone on in my past and the current situation I was in. I poured out my whole being to him. I would have been better off telling a rock. After I finished, I waited for what I thought would be a word of encouragement.

"When we are done building the church next door, I want you to help with the bulletin." He said nothing of what I had said to him. It was like the previous fifteen minutes never happened. I sat patiently listening to him talk about the new church. I could have cared less about the new church. Old feelings crept back in. After the meeting he walked my kids and I to my car. After I got into the car, he leaned down to my window. "I would like to meet with you without your kids one of these days." His suggestion made me feel uneasy. I did not know how to take it. I looked at him and smiled.

"Maybe." He moved away from the care and I left. I dropped the kids off at their daycare and went to work. I was still confused about the meeting. I could not understand how a man could call himself a man of God, and not listen to someone who is lost in the darkness. I lost hope. I could not understand it. I reasoned for hours within myself. I asked people at work about it. They could not understand it, either. When Deondre' got home from work, he called me at my job.

"Well, what did your pastor say?" He seemed anxious to hear what he had to say.

"After the new church is built, he wants me to help with the bulletin." I paused.

"That's all he said?"

"Yep," I said.

"You don't think something is wrong with that?"

"I don't know and I don't care." I ended the conversation and hung up the phone. I did not tell Deondre' what the pastor had said after I got into my car. I thought I might be over exaggerating. I did not want to upset him.

That Wednesday I went to bible study. The pastor asked, again, to see me without the kids. I felt uneasy about it. I tried to push the thoughts out of my head. I agreed to meet him the next day. I told Deondre' the pastor wanted to see me. He did not seem to be troubled with it. I did not give him the details of how the pastor wanted to meet. I still thought it was just myself over exaggerating. I wrestled with my thoughts all through the night. I had a bad feeling about the whole thing. It was the same bad feeling I always got just before something bad happened. I decided I would bring my kids. I also decided to show up conveniently late. I picked up my son from school before I went to the church. I was a half hour late. The pastor was about to pull off when I pulled up. He put his truck in gear, got out and walked over to my car.

"I didn't think you were coming." He was leaning down to the driver's side window.

"I had to pick up my son from school and I have to drop the kids off at daycare so I can go to work." For some reason, I was extremely nervous.

"I wanted to meet with you alone. Maybe some other time?"

"That will be fine." I nervously smiled at him.

"Well, I'll let you go so you can go to work." He stepped away from the car. I pulled off. I did not trust his true intentions. My gut feeling was telling me something more was going on then I was willing to believe. I was becoming confused and disillusioned.

After hours of thought, I decided to ask Deondre's opinion about the whole matter. After I stumbled through my words for a few seconds, I was finally able to tell him. I was afraid. I did not want to falsely accuse him of anything. Deondre' only reaffirmed my fears. He received the same impression I was getting. I never returned to that church, but that did not stop the pastor. I started receiving calls from him at my home. He called at least once a day. On one occasion, he called me from out of town. He was on vacation. He told me he had gotten my children something and wanted to give it to them when he returned. I stopped answering my phone. About two to three weeks later the phone calls from the pastor stopped.

I was now without a church. I finally found something that meant something to me, and it was snatched out of my hands. I was led into the wilderness and left there. I did not know which way to turn. I knew if I took one step in the wrong direction I would be lost forever. For once in my life, I truly stood still. The first lesson I learned from God was that I was no longer in control of my life. God taught me that any decision I made without Him would end miserably. It was a lesson I did not understand until much later. God was waiting for the perfect opportunity to put me in the perfect environment to hear the very word he would send forth for me to become saved the way he wanted me to be saved. Yes, I was supposed to go to church the day I got the overwhelming feeling to go. I just chose the wrong church.

Deondre' and I got a long fine as long as we did not talk about biblical matters. We had two completely different views. I grew up in a Baptist atmosphere and he grew up in an Apostolic atmosphere. This was all we needed. Actually, this was all God needed. God used reverse psychology on me. God used my own trick on me. I did not realize it until almost a year later. I can laugh about it now. I have always loved to argue my opinion to anyone who disagreed with me. I was very competitive when it came to proving someone wrong. One day as Deondre' and I talked, our conversation turned toward his church. The mild conversation turned into a full-blown argument. On his way out of the car to return to work from his lunch break he made the ultimate mistake.

"If you don't believe me, call my Bishop. Ask him." I could tell by the look on his face, he did not expect me to do it.

"No problem," I said with a smile. Deondre' looked at me strangely and walked into the building where he worked. When I got back to the house, I called Deondre's church and set up an appointment with his Bishop. I waited all day to tell Deondre' the news. When I finally picked him up, I blurted out what I had done. His eyes grew larger and larger as my words left my lips.

"What!" Deondre' became nervous.

"You heard me. I made an appointment to see your Bishop."

"No, you didn't. Stop. You didn't call." He became increasingly nervous.

"You told me to do it. So I did. I told you never to dare me. My appointment is Tuesday."

"Oh boy, I'm in trouble now. You weren't supposed to call him."

"Why are you so worried?"

"You don't know the Bishop. You'll see." Deondre's nervousness caused me to be nervous, but I knew I was doing the right thing no matter the outcome.

Tuesday came quickly. I went to the appointment with a new optimism. Deondre's Bishop had a lot to prove to me. I wanted resolution from what happened at the other church. I wanted answers for my questions. I had grown weary of people, and trusted no one. I especially did not trust clergy. I arrived at the church a little early. Deondre's mom worked at the daycare next door and came over to meet me. She had never met me before that time. I was Deondre's secret. She talked with me for a while before the Bishop called me into his office. I had imagined the Bishop as a small man like I have seen in Catholic churches. When he came out of his office I was quite surprised. He almost scared me. His appearance demanded respect in every sense. I sheepishly followed him into his office. He asked one of the assistants in the office to watch my kids for me. After talking with him for only a few minutes I could tell he was a man of intelligence and knowledge. I was greatly impressed.

A new door was opened for me. I was beginning my journey with God, again. The Bishop invited me to come back to one of the services the church offered. I left his office in a good spirit. A week later I started going on a regular basis. Deondre' was nervous about me attending his church, but he had no argument now. The Bishop had invited me to the church. I was going whether Deondre' liked it or not. I was excited. I was not going to allow him to kill my spirit. I was overwhelmed. I cannot explain the feelings exactly. It was like losing something precious and finding it unexpectedly. I had found the piece of the puzzle that completed the picture. It was the piece I had been looking for a very long time. I was baptized and received the Holy Ghost on June 9, 1999. My life has not been the same since.

CHAPTER EIGHT

"If so be that ye have heard Him, and have been taught by Him,
As the truth is in Jesus:
That ye put off concerning the former conversation the old man,
Which is corrupt according to deceitful lusts.
And be renewed in the spirit of your mind;
And that ye put on the new man,
Which after God is created in righteousness and true holiness."

Ephesians 4:21-24

****

A mechanic was working on a car. It had taken him hours to put a new part into the vehicle. When he was almost finished, he noticed he needed another part to finish the job. He left the garage to go to a parts store to find the part. While he was gone another mechanic came in for the first time that day. He noticed the car the first mechanic was working on was still jacked up. He walked over to the car. He was unaware the other mechanic had removed the old part and replaced it with the new part. He looked at the work order to see if he could help and then under the hood to see if the first mechanic had removed the part yet. Knowing it was a difficult part to remove and replace, he took the new part out. Upon return of the first mechanic, the second mechanic told him that he had taken the part out for him. The original mechanic became so angry he fired the second mechanic.

When we do things to help God, we do things we should not do. God is the original mechanic. He has been around since the beginning of the job. He knows what new parts we need and what parts have been replaced. If we go in and try to help God, we only make things worse.

> *"Being confident of this very thing,*
> *That he which hath begun a good work in you*
> *Will perform it until the day of Jesus Christ."*

Philippians 1:6

Our other problem is some of us need to realize we need some work to be done on us. The mechanic will not work on our car unless we take it to his garage. God does the same thing. God will not help unless we come to him and ask for assistance. Of course, we might think we know what the problem is, but like any good mechanic, God can tell just by the noise we are making what is wrong.

> *"…Your Father knoweth what things ye have need of, before ye ask*
> *him."*

Mathew 6:8

Are you letting God rebuild your life or are you trying to assist him in the repairs?

****

"Oh God, if only I could imagine the thoughts you have stored in one molecule of our existence, I would know all I could have ever imagined. Oh, if the words could enter my mind and leave through my fingers. If I could write what you breathe into my soul, I would have accomplished all I ever needed to. You have opened my eyes to a world of endless possibilities. You filled my body with joy unspeakable. You have cleansed my mind with peace. You covered my heart in the warmth of your love. You stand me up like a soldier when I fall. Your touch burns, but it heals. Thank you for having faith in me." I know my life exists in God. I know he has a purpose for my life. Our endless pursuit for his knowledge, wisdom and love begins when we stop looking.

"Be still and know that I am God..."

Psalm 46:10

People are told if they ever become lost in the woods to stop where they are and wait for someone to find them. I hear people say all the time after they become saved that they found God. How could they have found God if they were the ones that were lost? I was desperately lost. I had wondered the wilderness on my own for countless years. All I ever did was walk in circles. I was going nowhere. I wore myself down to a shell of a person. I was full of hate and anger. It had eaten away all that was of any good in me. I had no choice but to stop where I was and wait. I had no strength of my own any longer. I had no choice but to cry out for help hoping someone would come to my rescue. God met me where I was. He brought me out of the dark place I had put myself.

God does not always deliver us the way we want to be delivered. We always want the easy way out. If God always gave us the easy way out of a situation, we would never come to know him intimately. It is a known fact that people who go through war, tragedies, or disasters together develop a unique bond. God wants to develop this same unique bond with us, also. The only way this can happen is if God walks us through a situation instead of delivering us from it instantly. After I had become saved I expected all my wounds to be healed. They were not. I still had all the hate, hurts, and anger that I had bottled up within myself over the years. I could not understand why. I wanted the miraculous healing that everyone else testified about. I wanted instantaneous healing for wounds that were over thirty years old.

The most painful thing a person could experience is healing both physical and emotional. Wounds are painful. Sometimes, due to the pain we are in, we cannot focus on other things. If the wound is bad enough it could halt our normal activity. It could keep us from living a normal life. Wounds can become infected needing further treatment. Wounds leave visible and not so visible scars. In time, with proper treatment, most physical wounds will heal. The same is true for emotional wounds. Emotional wounds are just as painful, just as life halting and just as likely to become infected as physical wounds. They, also, can leave visible and not so visible scars, and in time, with the proper treatment, emotional wounds will heal too. The deeper the wound the longer it will take to heal.

I had to heal. I had to let God reopen old infected wounds to clean the poison out in order for them to heal properly. I did not want to do this. I did not want to feel that pain over again. I wanted it all to go away. I was tired of being in pain, but the one thing I did not realize was that the pain was a process I had to go trough. I never dealt with the pain before. I drowned the pain in anger, hate, and painkillers. I covered it up with a band-aid and went on my way. I let the wounds become infected and fester. I let the infection consume my entire life until it took over. God began treating my wounds one by one. He stitched up deep ones and put antiseptic on little ones. My wounds slowly started to heal, but this time they were healing properly. The deeper wounds are still healing, but the pain is gone. I have gone through the worst part. God has taught me patience in time of pain. He taught me it takes time to heal. Not all things come easily.

> *"Behold, we count them happy which endure.*
> *Ye have heard of the patience of Job,*
> *And have seen the end of the Lord;*
> *That the Lord is very pitiful, and of tender mercy."*

James 5:11

Before I could love God the way he intended, I had to learn to love. It was my deepest wound. It is a wound most of us tend to ignore. We find a definition of love that protects us. We do not fully understand the agape love God intends for us to experience. I lost the physical ability to truly love. I was not aware of this. God had to teach me to love without inhibition. God placed a special person in my life. It was not what I expected. It was a relationship that grew out of nothing into a beautiful union between two people. In the world I would have never allowed myself to love someone so dearly. I probably would have even wondered if something was wrong with me. You ask, why? The person God placed in my life is a beautiful woman of God. She was the first person I ever opened up to. She was the first person I felt safe with. God let me know her spirit was of his and she would never hurt me.

It was not through her love for me, but through my love for her that God showed me what pure love really was. Through my tears when she was in pain, through my want to do whatever she had asked of me, and through the endless hours she spent letting me speak to her, I learned to love. Through my love for her I learned the love God has for me. I would have never known the pure uninhibited unending agape love God has for me if God did not place her in my life. Just that one act of God has changed my life for eternity.

"…The soul of Jonathan was knit with the soul of David,
And Jonathan loved him as his own soul."

1 Samuel 18:1

Experiencing that kind of love for someone is experiencing the same kind of love God has for us.

"The Lord hath appeared of old unto me, saying,
Yea, I have loved thee with an everlasting love:
Therefore with lovingkindness have I drawn thee."

Jeremiah 31:3

As I look back over my life, it amazes me that I am still alive. After all the times I was beaten, tried to commit suicide, drove intoxicated, and took one more pill to take the edge off, I cannot believe I still have breath in my lungs. God did not consider my ways. He considered the ultimate goal. God did not judge me. He showed me mercy. I was guilty. God pardoned me. If it were not for God's mercies and grace I would not be here. God was the one who kept the knife from cutting too deeply. God kept the pills from poisoning my blood. God drove my car when I was too intoxicated to even see straight. The more I wanted to give up the more God pushed me to go on.

God never gave me the spirit of shame. I know the things I have done were wrong. I cannot change the past. I can only learn from it. I look at my mom, whom I love dearly. Growing up I tried to pattern my life after hers. I believed she was headed in the right direction.

"There is a way which seemeth right unto a man;
But the end thereof are the ways of death."

Proverbs 14:12

The relationship my mom had with my father had scarred her. It took my mom a long time to heal from that relationship. It took me a long time to realize I was following someone else's path and not my own. I am the survivor of five abusive relationships over a span of twenty-eight years of my life. The worst relationship I had was the one I had with myself. There is nothing more destructive than a person who cannot bear who they are or have become. It would have been very easy to blame God for every bad experience I had. Then I remember it would have been easier for God to snatch me out of existence.

> *"The grass withereth, the flower fadeth:*
> *Because the spirit of the Lord bloweth upon it:*
> *Surely the people is grass."*

Isaiah 40:7

I know God is not finished with me. I would be foolish to think he was. I have come to the conclusion that I rather wait on God. Everything I have done failed miserably. The decisions I made cost me more than a decade of precious time. Precious time I will never get back. When we are young, we do not realize how easily time will slip from us. We do not understand how precious life really is. When we are young, we do not think about the consequences we will face for our decisions. Sometimes even the smallest thing a person does can cause the most life altering changes to occur within their lives and the lives of others. When we are young, we do not realize our actions affect other people too. Every thought entertained has an action. Every action has a reaction. Every spoken word has a response. Everything goes back from where it came from. Everything we do will eventually find its way back to us. Our time on earth is valuable. It is valuable because we are only here for a short time. Our lives are like the flicker of a flame. It is brief and easily missed.

"As for man his days are as grass:
As a flower of the field so he flourisheth.
For the wind passeth over it, and it is gone;
And the place thereof shall know it no more."

Psalm 103:15,16

I suffered things I did not have to suffer. I stepped away from people who really wanted to help me. There is a disease called pride that infects people if they let it. It is a disease that silently takes over. It slowly consumes a person until it is too late. It affects our ability to think properly. It affects our ability to act properly. It causes us to do things we would not normally do if it had not infected us. I let pride infect me. Pride is what ruined my life. Almost everything I have been through has been the result of pride. Pride in its smallest form is detrimental if it is not stopped in time.

"Thy terribleness hath deceived thee, and the pride of thine heart,
O thou that dwellest in the clefts of the rock,
That holdest the height of the hill:
"Though thou shouldest make thy nest as high as the eagle,
I will bring thee down from thence, saith the Lord."

Jeremiah 49:16

It is a process of healing to admit we are wrong and need help. Everyone has done wrong in his or her lifetime. Everyone has need of help at one time or another. Our perfect source of help invites us to come to Him to receive the help we need.

"Come unto me, all that labor and are heavy laden, and I will give
you rest."

Mathew 11:28

The invitation has been sent. It is up to us to come. It is up to us to take the first step toward the source of our help, the Lord Jesus Christ.

"Let us therefore come boldly unto the throne of grace,
That we may obtain mercy, and find grace to help in time of need."

Hebrews 4:16

This book was not easy for me to write. Matter of fact, ninety percent of this chapter has been changed more than ten times. It was hard for me to come to the realization of who I was. This was one of the stitches I needed to heal a few of the deep wounds that consumed my life. God has blessed me to be able to express my feelings through written word. This humbles me. I do not feel I am worthy of such a great honor. I will never feel worthy, but I will continue to do his will. God has shown me through my weaknesses he will be glorified. He has shown me I am precious in his sight.

"Since thou wast precious in my sight,
Thou hast been honorable,
And I have loved thee…"

Isaiah 43:4

AFTERWORD

I want to express my love for the people involved in this book. I know a few discouraging words were said about a lot of people involved in my life. I did not write this book to have them judged for their actions or condemned for the things they have done. They were only responding to what I was doing to them. They are every bit deserving of God's love as I am. I have made amends with quite a few of the people in this book. I have apologized to my family. My love for them has grown deeper. I understand the things they did. My second son's grandmother and I have grown closer over time. She helps as much as she can. She has even become a foster grandmother for my daughter. The person I called Marquis was saved on my one-year anniversary date of becoming saved. He was even saved in the very same church as me. He and I are friends, now. God has since blessed my friend, who had turned her back on him, with a baby girl and a husband who loves her for who she is.

I want to thank you for reading this book. I pray that it has been a blessing for you to read. I know it has been a blessing for me to write. I pray that if you have not surrendered your life to Jesus Christ that you will. Or if you have gotten lost a long the way, I pray that you will let Jesus guide you back to the fold. I love you all because you are my brothers and sisters.

Again, I thank you.

If you are in trouble now and need help, there are plenty of agencies that can help you. They are listed in your phone book. Don't be afraid to let them help you. I will, also, leave the name of the church that has helped me grow in Christ over the past two years and my e-mail address.

Calvary Christian Church
939 Massachusetts Avenue
Pensacola, FL 32505
(850) 432-3902
www.calchristian.org

Jennifer M Killby
ruthsloyalty@cs.com